FOOD IN THE UNITED STATES, 1890–1945

Recent Titles in
Food in American History

American Indian Food
Linda Murray Berzok

Food in Colonial and Federal America
Sandra L. Oliver

Food in the United States, 1820s–1890
Susan Williams

FOOD IN THE UNITED STATES, 1890–1945

MEGAN J. ELIAS

Food in American History

GREENWOOD PRESS
An Imprint of ABC-CLIO, LLC

A B C 🟢 C L I O

Santa Barbara, California • Denver, Colorado • Oxford, England

Library of Congress Cataloging-in-Publication Data

Elias, Megan J.
    Food in the United States, 1890–1945 / Megan J. Elias.
        p. cm. — (Food in American history)
    Includes bibliographical references and index.
    ISBN 978-0-313-35410-6 (hard copy : alk. paper) — ISBN 978-0-313-35411-3 (ebook)
1. Food—History—19th century.   2. Food habits—United States—History—
19th century.   3. Cookery, American—History—19th century.   4. Food—
History—20th century.   5. Food habits—United States—History—20th century.
6. Cookery, American—History—20th century.   I. Title.
    TX355.E44   2009
    394.1'20973—dc22   2009012242

13 12 11 10 9   1 2 3 4 5

This book is also available on the World Wide Web as an eBook.
Visit www.abc-clio.com for details.

ABC-CLIO, LLC
130 Cremona Drive, P.O. Box 1911
Santa Barbara, California 93116-1911

This book is printed on acid-free paper ∞

Manufactured in the United States of America

CONTENTS

SERIES FOREWORD

This series focuses on food culture as a way to illuminate the societal mores and daily life of Americans throughout our history. These volumes are meant to complement history studies at the high school level on up. In addition, Food Studies is a burgeoning field, and foodies and food scholars will find much to mine here. The series is comprehensive, with the first volume covering American Indian food and the following volumes each covering an era or eras from Colonial times until today. Regional and group differences are discussed as appropriate.

Each volume is written by a food historian who is an expert on the period. Each volume contains the following:

- Chronology of food-related dates
- Narrative chapters, including
  Introduction (brief overview of period as it relates to food)
  Foodstuffs (staples, agricultural developments, etc.)
  Food Preparation
  Eating Habits (manners, customs, mealtimes, special occasions)
  Concepts of Diet and Nutrition (including religious strictures)
- Recipes
- Period illustrations
- Glossary, if needed
- Bibliography
- Index

CHRONOLOGY

1893   U.S. Supreme Court designates tomato a vegetable "for trade purposes."

World's Columbian Exposition opens in Chicago.

1896   *The Boston Cooking-School Cook Book,* by Fannie Merritt Farmer, is published.

1898   America is at war with Spain. U.S. soldiers reportedly are sickened by canned meat rations.

Chemist John T. Torrance develops condensed soup, making it easier to package. The Joseph P. Campbell Co. is established.

Hawaii becomes a territory of the United States. Puerto Rico becomes a possession of the United States.

1899   Minor Keith, an American who exports bananas from Costa Rica, and Boston Fruit Company, which exports bananas from Jamaica, merge to become United Fruit Company.

1900   20 percent of U.S. manufacturing product is food.

Good Housekeeping Research Institute opens with a test kitchen.

1901   Philippine Islands becomes a U.S. territory.

1902   Horn and Hardart form a partnership and open the first automat in the United States, in New York City.

1903   James Dole first cans pineapple, making it much easier to export.

United Fruit introduces refrigerated containers on ships, allowing bananas to be imported from Guatemala.

The tea bag is patented.

1906   The National Pure Food and Drug Act is passed.

Prepared mayonnaise becomes available in markets.

Per capita ice cream consumption is almost one gallon per year.

1908   Chicago becomes the first city to issue a mandatory pasteurization law for milk.

1909   For the first time, Americans produce more beef than pork products.

Americans consume 2.4 pounds of cheese per capita.

1910   The first electric household toaster is introduced by Westinghouse.

1911   Crisco shortening is introduced.

The paper egg carton is invented in Canada.

1912   Polish scientist Casimir Funk introduces the term *vitamine*, which is later changed to *vitamin*.

1913   American scientist Elmer McCollum isolates vitamins A and B.

1915   American per capita sugar consumption is more than 85 pounds per year.

Corning introduces Pyrex cookware.

Bacon is sold packaged in slices for the first time.

1916   Nearly 90 percent of milk is now pasteurized.

1917   The United States enters World War I. Voluntary rationing limits use of meat, wheat, fat, and sugar.

1918   The worldwide influenza epidemic occurs.

Orange juice sales increase.

Kelvinator refrigerator is introduced.

1920s   The Hollywood Eighteen Day Diet becomes the most popular diet fad.

1920   Most bread consumed is produced by commercial bakeries.

The Eighteenth Amendment, banning production, sale, and consumption of alcohol, goes into effect.

1923	Good Humor bars are first sold to the public.
1925	Clarence Birdseye develops a method to freeze food.
1927	William Henry Hay, diet doctor, is appointed Health Director of the Sun-Diet Sanatorium in East Aurora, New York.
1929	The stock market crash begins the Great Depression.
	7-Up is introduced.
1930	The Sunbeam Mixmaster is introduced.
1933	The Prohibition amendment is repealed by the Twenty-first Amendment.
1935	Edison Electric Institute and the National Electrical Manufacturers Association join forces "to actively promote kitchen modernization throughout the country."
1937	Spam is introduced by the Hormel company.
	The Waring blender (invented in 1922) is introduced to the market as an aid in making cocktails.
1941	America enters World War II. Voluntary rationing in the United States reduces consumption of meat, wheat, fat, and sugar.
	National Research Council Committee on Food and Nutrition and the Food and Drug Administration collaborate to introduce vitamin-enriched bread and flour to the American market.
1944	K rations are introduced to troops.
1945	World War II ends.
	Maxon Food Systems develops the first frozen airplane meal that could be reheated in flight.
1946	Per capita ice cream consumption is nearly five gallons per year.
	The National School Lunch Act is passed.

CHAPTER 1
INTRODUCTION

In the 1930s, the Federal Writer's Project Administration sent out a team of writers to discover what Americans were eating. As reports arrived back in Washington, D.C., the directors of the project experienced unexpected frustration; America's kitchens and community centers were full of foods of all nations proudly identified as regional specialties.[1] In some regions, what was celebrated as local cuisine was unabashedly commercial, rather than homemade. Was there such a thing as truly American food after all? Rather than exploring this fascinating question, the project's editors made their own decisions about which foods belonged to which region, cutting out overlap and ignoring what did not suit their preconceived notions of authenticity. This book seeks to set aside the false assumptions those editors made many years ago in order to understand what Americans really ate and how they thought about it between the turn of the century and the end of World War II. In doing so, at times the term *foodways*, which describes not only what a group of people are likely to eat, but also the place of food within their culture, is used. For example, baseball foodways refers to Americans' expectation to have access to hotdogs, crackerjacks, and unshelled peanuts at any baseball stadium they may visit. They do not expect, nor do they seem to desire, the tea and cakes associated with watching cricket matches in England. Another example might be that the foodways of urban Americans generally include purchasing meat that has been butchered into smaller pieces, rather than sold as a whole carcass. This book, then, explores not just American food, but also American foodways.

In 1890, America was still predominantly a rural nation, with the majority of its population living close to their food sources and personally involved in the production and processing of foods. By 1920, the population had shifted into urban areas and Americans were increasingly distanced from knowledge of their food's origins. By 1945, the nation was on the verge of another population shift as a surge of postwar construction established suburbs around most major cities and supermarkets became important food sources for a growing number of families. At the same time that Americans moved away from their food sources, these sources moved farther from them. Food was, increasingly, imported from other parts of the world to entice the palates of newly sophisticated Americans. Indeed, the farther they got from the original sources of their foods, the more diverse Americans' diets became. This was the result of improved methods of transportation for food and of the nation's expanded political and economic power. It was also the result of diverse cultures meeting for the first time in America's cities. Americans continue to experience both of these processes as the nation's food sources constantly increase in diversity while the country also continues to attract immigrants from all parts of the world who bring their food traditions and preferences with them.

Over the course of the period discussed in this book, what, where, when, and how Americans ate all changed. Technological advances brought electricity into the home, speeding up cooking times and making fresh produce available year round. Advances in food preservation also made it easier for Americans to prepare a wider range of foods, and decreasing family sizes meant that the family cook had fewer mouths to feed. The introduction of the automobile provided new means for transportation of food, as well as creating a new market for "road food" provided by diners and roadside stands to an increasing stream of travelers. The advent of commercial air travel in the 1930s introduced the nation to the dubious pleasures of airplane food.

The years between 1890 and 1945 were also a time marked by serious crises that affected what Americans could eat and changed their thinking about everyday meals. For example, soldiers who had served in Europe during World War I brought home new tastes, as well as a new awareness of America's food bounty. Those who lived through the shortages of the Great Depression typically did not look at food the same way again.

In 1893, when the Columbian Exposition opened in Chicago, visitors encountered a giant knight on horseback made entirely of prunes and an elephant made of walnuts, peanuts, oranges, and lemons. The exposition, which celebrated (one year late) the 450th anniversary of Columbus's arrival in the Americas, served as a showcase for American wealth and food innovation. Shredded wheat and cream of wheat cereals both made their debuts at the exposition, where their inventors attempted to convince fairgoers that whole grains were not only healthy but also tasty. The Rumford Kitchen, designed by chemist Ellen Richards, similarly sought to educate consumers by providing them with simple wholesome meals. Named in honor of Count Benjamin Rumford, who had been one of the world's first nutritionists, the kitchen not only served lunch but also provided diners with printed information about the nutritional aspects of their meal.

Less didactic than the Rumford Kitchen and less spectacular than the food sculptures but nevertheless appealing, the restaurants and food stalls associated with the exhibits of foreign nations and American regions offered such exotic treats as the shark's fin and bird's nest soup found at the Chinese Café.[2] At the San Antonio Chili Stand, many visitors encountered chili—a creation of the Mexican American borderlands—for the first time, setting off a nationwide interest in the dish.[3]

The wide variety and great quantity of food found at the exposition reflected two trends in American society during the 1890s: improved agricultural production and expanded U.S. political influence in the Caribbean, Central America, and the Pacific. Advances in farming technology and transportation methods had increased the amount of food that farmers could produce and expect to sell, resulting in lowered prices through the 1890s. Agricultural populists organized to try to solve these problems collectively and one, Mary Lease, was quoted as advising that farmers should "raise more hell and less corn," in order to regulate the market in their favor.[4]

As farmers struggled with falling prices and corporate control of transportation, some American businessmen developed agricultural empires outside U.S. borders. New Yorker Minor Keith, who originally invested in railroads in Costa Rica, found that he could make more money selling the bananas that grew alongside his train tracks than he could running trains. The United Fruit Company, created in 1899 when Keith merged his company with the Boston Fruit Company, which had plantations in the West Indies, benefited hugely from the introduction of refrigerated shipping containers in 1903.[5] Even before this time, the company was so large and well organized that the government of Guatemala contracted with it to run the nation's postal service. In Hawaii, a group of American-run sugar corporations known as the Big Five came to dominate both the economy and the politics of the territory early in the 20th century. Frequently, territorial governors had previously served as agents of one of the five companies that controlled the sugar market.[6]

In 1898, America became involved in a war with Spain over that country's imperial possessions in the Caribbean. The war soon spread to include Spanish possessions in the Pacific. Although the official explanation for the war was that Spain had sunk an American warship in Havana, Cuba, the U.S. government also had a strong interest in becoming the only major power in the region. As American businessmen established trade relationships with fruit plantation owners, the U.S. government became more and more interested in making sure that Caribbean governments were friendly to them. As a result of the war, the United States annexed Puerto Rico and Hawaii and made the Philippines a U.S. territory.

In 1901, soon after Hawaii was annexed, a young American named James Dole settled there and began to grow pineapples for export. By 1922, he was able to purchase an entire island, creating the world's largest plantation. It certainly did not hurt his business interests that his cousin Sanford Dole had been president of the Republic of Hawaii, having participated in removing the native Queen Lili'uokalani in 1893.

While American business interests expanded through the Caribbean and Pacific resulting in new foods imported, new immigrants from Europe brought their traditional foods and foodways to America, importing from the old country when they could and improvising with American foodstuffs when they could not. Between 1900 and 1921, more than 1 million immigrants arrived from Europe, settling mostly in the cities of the Northeast. Because many of these immigrants were Eastern European Jews who observed kosher dietary laws, they established their own markets in the cities to ensure cultural continuity with the past. Children's book author Sydney Taylor recounted an experience of one of these shops in the popular book *All-of-a-Kind Family:* "The chicken market was . . . smelly and noisy with the squawking of fowl. . . . Mama donned an apron she had brought with her and began to pluck the fowl she selected. After Mama finished her plucking, the chicken was wrapped up and added to the other bundles in the shopping bag."[7]

At the same time that these large numbers of Europeans were arriving in America, a movement of people within the nation known as the Great Migration, was beginning to occur, changing food practices. Fleeing racial violence and legalized discrimination in the South, approximately one-and-a-half million African Americans moved to northern cities between 1900 and 1940. As these migrants established new communities, they shared their foodways both with the preexisting population and with other migrants, discovering similarities and differences in traditional African American cuisine from different regions.[8] Visitors to Harlem's famous Cotton Club, where only white audiences were allowed, could experience exotic southern treats such as barbecued spareribs while they simultaneously gained an introduction to new music and dance forms.

The interest in food as fuel that inspired the Rumford Kitchen at the Columbian Exposition in 1893 led to the discovery of vitamins in the 1910s by scientists working separately and in collaboration in the United States, Japan, and Europe. Now nutritionists, a new kind of specialist, could begin to tell Americans what they needed to eat in order to become and stay healthy. Having already identified the basic elements of food—fats and starches—nutritionists and dietitians could begin to design balanced diets. The U.S. Congress also supported the movement toward a more healthy diet for Americans when it passed the Pure Food and Drug Act in 1906. Partly inspired by author Upton Sinclair's graphic portrait of unsanitary conditions in meatpacking plants in the novel *The Jungle,* the act provided federal inspection of food processing plants and raised standards for packaging information.

Also concerned with national health, men and women of the temperance movement finally succeeded in banning alcohol production and consumption, with the passage of the Eighteenth Amendment in 1919. Far from eliminating liquor from American's lives, Prohibition, as the amendment has come to be known, opened up the drinking life to an expanded clientele, as drinks were consumed in secret venues. These places were known as speakeasies because the patrons need not be afraid of being caught and could thus "speak easy" about their illegal drinking. That much of the liquor served in such places was homemade and harsh-tasting led to the popularization of the cocktail—a type of drink first created in the early 19th century that mixed alcohol with various flavors and beverages to make it more palatable. To cover for their illegal operations, some speakeasies also served food, introducing new sectors of society to the pleasures of dining out, previously a treat reserved for wealthy businessmen. Hotels, which had enjoyed large profits from their onsite bars, now found that the only way to keep profits up was to expand their food offerings and transform barrooms into restaurants.

In 1917, when America entered World War I, food conservation became an important issue. The U.S. Food Administration published and distributed material that told Americans which foods to scrimp on and how to prepare tasty meals from what was left. Voluntary conservation allowed the nation not only to feed its own troops but also to supply its allies and, once the war was over, to help feed European war survivors whose agricultural land had been devastated by four years of combat.[9] Meanwhile, American soldiers serving in France and Italy had experienced some of the pleasures of European cuisines for the first time and could not quite forget these flavors when they returned home.

The decade after World War I was one of prosperity and plenty for America. Road building and advances in automotive technology made it possible for food to travel greater distances, while new systems of credit purchasing made it possible for those without much cash to acquire new kitchen appliances. As migration from rural areas increased urban populations, restaurants opened in growing numbers to serve working men and women who could not travel home for lunch. Although even most urban dwellers still ate dinner at home during the 1920s, the new nightlife of speakeasies and movie theaters increased the demand for restaurants to stay open for dinner.

In the rural areas that many of the new city dwellers had left behind, a major shift in food production was reaching a critical point that divides the agriculture of today from that of millennia before. Beginning in the late 19th century, food production had begun this shift away from production for family use to production for sale to a national market. The motto "Go big or get out" applied to farmers of this era to devastating effects for many who were unable to make the change from a wide variety of produce grown on a small plot of land to a single crop grown on many hundreds of acres. The transition required new machinery, larger parcels of land, and new attention to transportation of goods to market.

While farms grew larger and fewer, corporations that processed food and agencies that advertised the new processed foods emerged in greater numbers and with new techniques for convincing consumers to buy. By 1900, food processing accounted for 20 percent of industrial production in the United States. Shoppers encountered brighter and more appealing labels on processed foods such as canned vegetables, fruits, and meats, as well as more attractive displays in the groceries they frequented.[10] Throughout the 1920s, most Americans bought their food from small, independently owned groceries where they typically paid for goods on credit, settling their bills once a month. Although larger grocery chains such as A&P were beginning to appear, they did not get the chance to expand until the Great Depression of the 1930s. When the Depression struck, many small grocers found they could no longer extend credit to customers who were less and less able to pay for purchases. Larger chain stores were able to use the fact that they could buy in bulk at a discount to lower their prices and attract customers during this time. Meanwhile, nutritionists attempted to reach impoverished Americans with vital information about how to maintain nutritious diets on reduced budgets. First Lady Eleanor Roosevelt even "modeled" budget meals at the White House, although only when no important guests were expected for dinner.

In the first years of the Great Depression, there was no shortage of food produced by American farmers; the problem was distribution. Overproduction because of good weather and improved farm technology meant that it was not cost-effective for farmers to get their goods to market. Lost jobs and lowered incomes also made it difficult for those who did not farm to afford the food that farmers produced. In many rural areas and small towns, Americans returned to a barter economy, trading foods for services. In cities, relief agencies struggled

Until the 1920s, customers in most American country stores asked for items that were then taken down from the shelves by clerks. These stores stocked a wide range of items other than foods. (AP Photo.)

This Piggly Wiggly market in Tennessee, c. 1918, was in the first generation of self-service groceries. (Courtesy of Library of Congress.)

to feed hungry families while single people waited in breadlines for whatever charities could distribute. In the middle years of the crisis, drought and resulting dust storms in the central plains caused many farmers who had survived on what they could grow to abandon their farms or starve to death.

The food shortages of the depression mostly ended in 1939 with the beginning of World War II in Europe. Although the United States was not involved as a combatant until 1941, national industries were revived to supply America's traditional allies, Britain and France, with food and military supplies. Hired on at reopened factories, city dwellers could now afford to buy the food that farmers could now afford to produce. Just as in World War I, the U.S. government asked for voluntary rationing once the nation became involved in the war. Housewives, for example, were asked to save grease because meat fats could be turned into glycerin, an important ingredient in bullets. Soldiers, sailors, and marines of the U.S. military serving in Europe and the Pacific were fed on food packages developed by nutritionist Ancel Keys. Known as K rations, the packages came in three varieties—breakfast, lunch, and dinner—and although rated "better than nothing," by the soldiers who consumed them first in a taste test, they never won any culinary awards. As one journalist noted: "Many a soldier will remember the mud and the K-rations long after the memory of danger has grown dim."[11]

Rounded up as alien enemies during the war, Japanese Americans attempted to preserve food traditions in internment camps on the West Coast. This was difficult because supplies were brought to the camps with no consideration of Japanese food traditions. As one older woman complained "I can't stand the food. Don't they know Japanese people need more fresh fruit and vegetables?"[12] Internees were eventually successful in getting authorities to replace potatoes with rice, a staple of their cooking, and some secretly managed to continue brewing sake, traditional Japanese liquor, from leftover rice.

By the end of the war in 1945, America was entering a new phase of prosperity in which food scarcity would no longer threaten large numbers of people. With a population shift into newly built suburbs, supermarkets would displace small independent markets, changing both food supply and demand. Meanwhile, a heightened sense of themselves as citizens in a global economy would gradually increase American interest in the cuisines of other nations. Increased numbers of families with disposable income would also lead to the proliferation of restaurants throughout the towns and cities of America. The affordable automobile that made suburban living possible would also lead to a burgeoning new market in "fast food" that has come to be associated internationally with America.

NOTES

1. Donna Gabaccia, *We Are What We Eat* (Cambridge, MA: Harvard University Press, 1998), pp. 139–44. The project known as "America Eats" was never published because the U.S. entry into World War II shifted governmental priorities. Pieces of the project exist in state archives and some have been published in Nelson Algren, *America Eats* (Iowa City: University of Iowa Press, 1992).

2. Mae Ngai, "Transnationalism and the Transformation of the Other: Response to the Presidential Address," *American Quarterly* 57, no. 1 (2005): 62.

3. Gabaccia, *We Are What We Eat*, p. 109.

4. Although the statement is widely attributed to Lease, it seems to have been a paraphrase or even a misattribution rather than a direct quotation. In an article in the *Topeka State Journal*, May 25, 1896, Lease claimed that she never said the phrase but allowed herself to be misquoted because the spirit of the statement seemed correct to her.

5. Sarah Murray, *Moveable Feasts* (New York: St. Martin's Press, 2007), p. 103.

6. John S. Whitehead, "Western Progressives, Old Southern Planters, or Colonial Oppressors: The Enigma of Hawai'i's 'Big Five,' 1898–1940" *The Western Historical Quarterly* 30, no. 1 (1999): 295–326.

7. Sydney Taylor, *All-of-a-Kind Family* (New York: Dell Publishing, 1989), pp. 74–75.

8. John Brown Childs, "Afro-American Intellectuals and the People's Culture," *Theory and Society* 13, no. 1 (1984): 81.

9. See Harvey Levenstein's chapter on food and World War I, "Food Will Win the War," in *A Revolution at the Table* (Berkeley: University of California Press, 2003).

10. See William Leach, "Strategies of Enticement," pp. 15–111 in *Land of Desire* (New York: Random House, 1993) for a discussion of the development of commercial window displays.

11. "GIs Resented Privileges," *Science News Letter,* May 28, 1949.

12. Mary Matsuda Gruenewald, *Looking Like the Enemy: My Story of Internment in Japanese American Internment Camps* (Troutdale, OR: New Sage Press, 2005), p. 56.

CHAPTER 2
FOODSTUFFS

The ingredients of American meals began to change significantly at the end of the 19th century as America expanded its territories around the world and new technologies made it possible to transport the delicacies of all regions to all other regions fresh throughout the year. Changing availability helped to change tastes even as traditional flavors and preparations remained popular. Expanding possibilities broadened the national palate to include foodstuffs and dishes that 19th-century eaters had not known. What had once been exotic became expected as Americans began to learn the pleasures of eating more globally.

In 1896, Fannie Merritt Farmer published what was to become the most influential cookbook in American history. Farmer's *Boston Cooking-School Cook Book* introduced American cooks to the concept of level measurements and made a strong argument for thinking about food in terms of physical health as well as pleasure. She began her cookbook by defining food in scientific terms and looked forward to the day when "a knowledge of the principles of diet will be an essential part of one's education." When that day came, "mankind will eat to live, will be able to do better mental and physical work, and disease will be less frequent."[1]

The book, which has never been out of print and has been revised many times over the years, included dishes that were considered national standards. Farmer did not attempt to introduce her readers to new cuisines. Her goal was to help them prepare their favorites reliably well. Despite the enduring popularity of the book, now published as the *Fannie Farmer Cookbook,* the 50 years after its publication were marked by increased interest in the cuisines of the world and also in the growing use of processed foods. As one cooking teacher and author declared in 1914, "American cookery has become cosmopolitan in its character. The New England cookery of colonial time has been superseded by cookery that has culled the best from every land and clime."[2]

This chapter looks at the change and continuity in what Americans ate. The dominant culture in the United States traced its foodways back to northern Europe, but other groups, such as people of Central American ancestry and those of African ancestry also experienced change in their foodways. One Mexican American woman who had grown up in Detroit, Michigan, for example, commented in 1945 that among her family "they do not have as many Mexican dishes as they used to." Mexican cuisine was reserved for special occasions. She attributed this to the fact that "American food is so much more easily prepared," so her family "have succumbed to it to a greater extent than we would have if flavor alone was the factor." In other words, her family did not eat American food because they liked it better but because it was harder to find Mexican food staples in Detroit.[3]

MEATS

Although ordinary people have not always had access to large quantities of it, meat has played an important role in American foodways since the arrival of the first European settlers. When they thought about a really good meal, the vast majority of Americans probably imagined at least one large piece of meat in the center of their ideal table. Foodways of the wealthy generally included a wide selection of meats—fish, fowl, and flesh—at each meal.

In earlier eras, pork had played a central role in American diets primarily because pigs were so easy to keep, feeding themselves on whatever they could find, and needing little maintenance. Cows were often raised for the dairy products through which they provided a return on the larger investment it took to contain and feed them. By the late 19th century, however, a major cattle industry had emerged in the American West, and the use of railroads and refrigerated rail cars made it possible for more Americans to eat beef. In 1909, for the first time, Americans produced more beef products, including veal, than pork. Beef production had increased 44 percent since 1899 and, although it experienced periods of increase and decline, remained well above 19th-century levels.[4] Some of this meat was purchased raw and prepared at home, but increasing amounts reached the consumer already processed in cans. The most famous American canned meat product, Spam, was introduced in 1937 by the Hormel Company. Hormel had already pioneered in the field of processed meat by introducing canned hams 11 years earlier. Spam was essentially a way to use up the leftovers of this process. Because it was made of pork, rather than beef, Spam was not rationed during World War II and thus was able to gain a wider audience. It was also very useful to the military, as it did not need to be refrigerated to stay edible.

For the very poor, red meat continued to be a rarity. As Pauline Fakes, an African American agricultural worker in Alabama remarked to an interviewer in the 1930s, "I don't have much cake. Little cornbread and meat, molasses and proud to get that."[5] Also in the 1930s, folklorist Zora Neale Hurston remembered a Florida childhood of abundance in which beef was still uncommon and highly prized: "We had chicken on the table often. . . . There was plenty of fish in the lakes around town, and so we had all we wanted. But beef stew was something rare. We were all very happy whenever Papa went to Orlando and came back with something delicious like stew beef. Chicken and fish were too common with us."[6]

At the end of the nineteenth and beginning of the 20th century, those who could afford it commonly consumed beef as steak, roast beef, stew, or in a traditional boiled dinner. Cookbook authors such as Fannie Farmer and Sarah Tyson Rorer also assumed that their readers would want to cook beef tripe, tongue, heart, and head, pieces of the animal that would become less popular in mainstream cookbooks over the course of the 20th century. A popular recipe of the turn of the century, beef a la mode, despite what modern readers might assume, did not involve ice cream but rather required inserting cubes of fatty pork, known as lardoons, into a piece of beef, which was then simmered in water for several hours with vegetables.[7] Veal also was a staple of cookbooks, served both as roast and, very commonly, as cutlets.

By the 1910s, American home cooks seemed to be preparing beef in smaller portions. An extreme version of this was the raw beef sandwich that appeared in the *Washington Women's Cookbook,* a book compiled to raise money for the suffragist cause: "Scrape lean round steak with a sharp knife. Spread the scraped meat on thin buttered bread; season with salt and pepper and cover with a piece of thin buttered bread."[8]

Informal and far from "ladylike," the recipe reflected the more active lifestyles of Americans during this era. The suffragists who sold this cookbook clearly hoped to spend more time involved in civic affairs than in the kitchen roasting big pieces of meat.

In 1913, the *American Food Journal* noted the "constant effort many housewives are making to supply their tables with food less expensive than meat." A "bright housekeeper" quoted in the article explained that the family "generally have meat twice a week . . . once as a basis for soup and again as a medium-priced pot roast for Sunday dinner." For other meals, she used beans, cheese, and pasta to supply the family's protein needs.[9]

During World War I, beef was rationed to provide adequately for American soldiers overseas. Several restaurant owners in New York City, however, took it upon themselves to exempt organ meats, or "internal delicacies" from the ration, only to find their restaurants closed temporarily by the Federal Food Board as punishment.[10] Soldiers on the front enjoyed rations that included fresh meat and vegetables as well as candy and cigarettes—a great improvement over the "embalmed beef" rations that nearly caused mutiny during the Spanish American War.

Cookbooks of the 1920s and 1930s introduced more recipes that involved minced, ground, or "chipped" beef, suggesting that one might make a roast once a week and use the leftovers to make other, lighter dishes. Croquettes and timbales appear to have been the preferred method of using up scraps through the 1940s. Croquettes mixed meat scraps with rice to form patties that were then dipped in egg and breading and then fried. Timbales mixed the scraps with egg, cream, and breading, and then steamed the mixture in specially designed cups. In the 1950s, casseroles would begin to take their place. The move from large pieces to small reflected growing informality in American family relations, as well as shrinking family sizes.

Beef and Rice Croquettes

To use up cold meat economically, combine two cups of chopped beef or mutton with freshly boiled rice. Season well with salt, pepper, onion juice, a large teaspoon of minced parsley, and a teaspoon of lemon juice. Pack on a large plate and set away to cool. After the mixture is cold, shape into croquettes, dip into beaten egg, roll in fine crumbs and fry in smoking hot fat.[11]

From the mid 19th century until the 1930s, pork was associated with the lower classes, so cookbooks, which were primarily directed at middle class audiences, did not provide many recipes for its use. Fannie Farmer declared it "the most difficult of digestion" and suggested "it should be but seldom served."[12] Mary Hinman Abel, writing a cookbook for people with little income, acknowledged that "say what we may against pork," its low cost made it "a most valuable kind of meat." That said, however, "it is of little use to give rules about buying this meat; we must take what the butcher furnishes." Beggars could not be connoisseurs.[13]

Arthur Davis, who came of age during the Harlem Renaissance, offered a different perspective on pork as food. Davis remembered that at parties during the 1920s, "there would be plenty of what we now call *soul-food:* chitterlings, pig feet, hopping-john, and similar delicacies."[14] Published cookbooks tended to reflect the foodways of the majority culture and mostly provided recipes for muscular cuts of meat, but cultures outside the mainstream celebrated other parts as "delicacies."

Sausages, a staple of 19th-century cookbooks, appeared in the 20th century primarily as premade, store-bought items to be incorporated into recipes rather than something to be made at home. A San Francisco grocer's catalog printed in 1909 offered 17 varieties of sausage for sale including both goose liver and nut.[15] By 1914, a popular cookbook began each recipe for sausage with the injunction to "prick the casings," assuming a ready-made product.[16]

As large cuts of beef became less popular, cookbook authors offered more chicken recipes. In 1924, an author identified several as appropriate for "formal" meals, reflecting a rise in the status of chicken, which had once been considered a food for the family alone or an addition to a larger feast and not to be served to guests as the centerpiece of a meal. Americans ate chicken prepared in a variety of ways—roasted, broiled, fried, and stewed. Very popular in middle class homes in the 1920s and 1930s were varieties of jellied chicken, which suspended chopped pieces of chicken in gelatin, creating something between a terrine and a Jello mold. Chicken fricassee, in which pieces of chicken were first fried and then stewed in cream, also seems to have remained a favorite through the end of World War II. Recipes for turkey appeared in most cookbooks, although it was not identified in particular with Thanksgiving as it might be today.

Before 1945, Americans ate a smaller variety of fish than they would toward the end of the century. This reflected the difficulty of transporting fresh fish inland and the lack of technology developed later that made deep-sea fishing feasible. With the exception of trout, cookbooks tended to give recipes only for saltwater fish such as salmon, cod, mackerel, and halibut. In reality, those who lived far from the sea certainly ate other freshwater fish such as bass, and catfish, typically prepared simply by rolling in corn meal or cracker crumbs and frying or sautéing in butter. Fish and seafood that could be canned, such as salmon, oysters, crabmeat, and even lobster, appeared in most cookbooks. By the 1920s, it was also common to find one or two recipes in cookbooks that used canned tuna. Canned seafood was usually prepared in croquettes or fritters and sometimes as part of a salad. Although overfishing and pollution had both drastically reduced the availability of oysters, cookbooks continued to print more recipes for ways to prepare them than for any other shellfish. Shipped in from purer waters, their prices rose and soon only the wealthy could eat them fresh. Portions also consequently declined and where diners once ate 20 or more fresh oysters at a time, cookbooks now recommended six per person.

During the crisis of the Great Depression, meat became increasingly scarce in American homes. A cookbook published in 1931 offered a chapter on meat substitutes: "In these days of the high cost of living it is wise to eliminate meat from the bill of fare for two or three days out of every week."[17] To make up for the loss of meat without substantially altering mainstream American foodways, the cookbook offered various "loafs" and "cutlets" and this recipe, for walnut scrapple:

> Cook one cupful of cornmeal and one-half cupful of hominy in one quart of salted boiling water for twenty minutes. Season with salt and pepper to taste; add one tablespoonful of melted butter, and one cupful of chopped walnuts or mixed nuts; then pour in a greased pan to mold and cool. When cold, cut into slices and fry. Serve with sirup [*sic*] or butter.[18]

Wild game, which some families relied on during the depression, became less a part of mainstream diets during the 20th century as Americans moved into cities and away from woodlands. Where 19th-century cookbooks listed recipes for saddleback ducks, hare, terrapins, and often squirrel, 20th-century cookbooks aimed at a middle class audience seldom included anything more exotic than duck or goose. Increasingly, cookbooks assumed that meats would come from butchers or grocers, rather than from the barnyard or forest. Where an 1899 cookbook included instructions on how to butcher fowl, a 1924 author noted that for those interested in cooking hare, "The hare, or rabbit, will be dressed for you at the market and may be cut into six or eight pieces."[19]

By the 1940s, game seems to have become food that marked the high status of elites. In New York, the E. Joseph, Inc. "luxury" grocery advertised in one cookbook marketed to urban sophisticates that they stocked "wild game from the world over," including English pheasants and reindeer roasts.[20] As domestic tourism increased in the

1940s, another cookbook created for outdoor adventurers revealed that most of the natural world was edible, daringly including recipes for crow, owl, and even skunk. It can be assumed that these delicacies were seldom sampled, especially among the target audience of the book—those with free time and disposable income necessary for camping trips. Rural Americans, however, did continue to consume wild game such as deer, squirrel, turtle, and possum as welcome supplements to sometimes meager diets. As described in one cookbook about regional American foodways, for example, "the typical cuisine of impoverished hillbillies and sharecroppers" was "wild berries, fruits, nuts, and game in season and chopped corn . . . to sustain life through the winter."[21]

VEGETABLES

From the end of the 19th century through the end of World War II, Americans ate vegetables either cold as salads or hot as dishes to accompany meat. Salads often served as lunch and hot vegetable dishes as dinner fare, but salads could also be used to start a formal meal and hot vegetable dishes served without meat for casual lunches. For Americans of the period before the 1960s, salad had a very broad meaning. One author noted, "Almost every kind of fish, meat, vegetable and fruit may be served as salad." What made a dish a salad was that it was served cold, composed carefully, even artistically on the plate, and typically involved lettuce leaves used as cups or garnish.[22] This was food for middle class American families in which women typically stayed at home and were responsible for all family meals. Elements of a salad were ordinarily bound together by dressing, usually a mayonnaise, often one fortified with cream. Mayonnaise was first available in groceries after 1906. Before this time, cooks had to make the emulsion themselves, a difficult task. Once a treat, mayonnaise could now be enjoyed every day, which perhaps accounts for its frequent use in salads during the 1910s. By 1928, more than 7 million gallons of mayonnaise were manufactured in the United States.[23] Cookbooks of the 1920s and 1930s were full of creative salads such as poinsettia salad (tomatoes and green peppers), sweetbread salad, and baked bean and tomato salad. One author cautioned against over-enthusiasm: "Many salads have been served under that name which should have been called cold hash . . . Do not try to see how many varieties of food you can use in combination; the choice salad consists of a few ingredients carefully chosen."[24] The author suggested that Americans as a people lacked subtlety when it came to salads, for "perfectly crisp and chilled salad greens with a piquant dressing are liked by the epicure better than the fanciful salads so much in demand in this country."[25] Usually, apart from the lettuce, salad vegetables had been cooked before being dressed. A general distrust of raw vegetables prevailed through the first half of the 20th century.

Beginning in the early years of the 20th century, commercially packaged gelatin offered another way to bind salad ingredients together. Although powdered gelatin had been available for more than 20 years and was used in main courses such as the previously mentioned jellied chicken, the fashion for using it to make salads did not become widespread until the 1920s. For those who considered the salad ideally to be a work of art, Jello offered exciting new possibilities. A typically exuberant salad of this era is the ginger ale aspic salad found in a 1939 cookbook. This salad called for suspending grapes, celery, crushed pineapple, and preserved ginger in a gelatin made with ginger ale, another commercial product. The salad was to be served in lettuce cups with a dressing of mayonnaise mixed with whipped cream.[26]

When Americans cooked vegetables, they usually boiled them, sometimes adding bicarbonate of soda to preserve color. Writing in 1932, an American cookbook author declared that "Potatoes rank first in importance in the vegetable line," a perspective that seems to have been shared by other writers throughout the period from the turn of the century to the end of World War II.[27] Some books even dedicated whole chapters to this well-loved tuber. In general, white potatoes were more popular in the North and West, whereas sweet potatoes were most commonly used in the South. Of the many suggested treatments for potatoes, most involved butter and many involved milk, "scalloping" and "creaming" being favorite ways to prepare this and all other vegetables. Creamed vegetables were served coated in white sauce, and scalloped vegetables were baked in the same sauce. One cookbook author cheerfully noted, "You can change your white sauce for each menu as you would your hat to match each outfit!"[28] While encouraging readers to cook vegetables for less time than was traditional, a writer for the *Woman's Home Companion* suggested that "it is still good practice to reduce the cooking odors by putting a slice of bread in the saucepan." The writer noted that although nutritionally cabbage, cauliflower, brussels sprouts and onions were "four of our best friends and strongest allies," they were "sometimes perhaps too strong!"[29] Commonly consumed vegetables included tomatoes, corn, beans—both dried and fresh—peas, cauliflower, and carrots.

In 1899, well-known food writer Christine Terhune Herrick used her syndicated newspaper column to lament, "few persons appreciate the full value of the tomato in the family bill of fare." Americans, Herrick noted, used the tomato to make salads or soup and perhaps served them scalloped or stewed. In doing so "they have hardly touched upon its possibilities." A plethora of recipes for white sauce-based tomato soup and for salads served in hollowed out tomatoes continued to support her analysis for many years after she made it. When Americans cooked tomatoes without milk and butter, these dishes tended to be identified as coming from foreign or regionally specific cultures, as with dishes such as Italian stew, baked tomatoes Creole style, and the Mexican tomatoes recipe that won a prize for Mrs. Harry Kleinfelter (possibly not a person of Mexican ancestry), of Hamilton Ohio in 1929.[30] Typically, canned tomatoes were used in cooked dishes and fresh tomatoes only in salads, where their bright colors contributed to the generally artistic effect of salads of the early 20th century. One example, the tomato and cheese salad, involved slicing a tomato, spreading each slice with cream cheese, and reconstructing the vegetable, which was then sprinkled with walnuts, dolloped with mayonnaise, and placed on a lettuce leaf for what was surely an impressive effect.[31]

Americans also used tomatoes to make relishes, although fewer and fewer made relishes and pickles at home. Where earlier generations of women had used tomatoes from their gardens to put up a supply of tomato ketchup for the winter, most who used ketchup in the 20th century bought it from grocers, where it had been commercially available since the 1870s. In general, homemade ketchup was somewhat chunky and rather spicy, having more in common with chutneys than with the smooth sauce that companies like Heinz offered. Experimentation in the early1900s eliminated the use of benzoate, used as a preservative, in commercial ketchup, which increased its popularity, as there were some concerns about the safety of this chemical in food. Around this time, the Heinz company purchased a recipe from a woman in Pennsylvania that produced a ketchup that was both sweeter and saltier and also denser than previous recipes.[32] A 1910 advertisement for Heinz emphasized its lack of benzoate "or other drugs," declaring "fresh material and clean preparation make drugs of any kind unnecessary in prepared foods." Consumers were encouraged to "protect yourself by reading all food labels carefully."[33]

The popularization of knowledge about vitamins gave nutritionists and recipe writers another reason to recommend tomatoes, as this fruit is high in vitamin C. By the 1920s, vitamin C was understood to be essential to good nutrition. Growing assimilation of Italian foodways into American culture also contributed to increased consumption of tomatoes, although often "Italian" dishes were not fully recognizable as such. Tomato sauces for dishes such as "macaroni a la Italienne" offered in a 1914 cookbook were made by mixing canned tomatoes into a flour-based sauce.[34]

Most cookbooks also provided one or two recipes for eggplant and often one for asparagus. Salsify, a root also known as oyster plant, and turnips appeared commonly through the 1920s and less so by the 1940s. Both were usually given the popular creaming or scalloping treatments.

Apart from cabbage, recipes for cooking leafy green vegetables do not seem to have been an important part of mainstream American foodways. A cookbook celebrating the diversity of African American cooking, however, included recipes for collard greens, beet greens, mustard greens, kale, and dandelion greens, reflecting a deep connection to the foodways of West Africa, where cooked greens are an important part of many cuisines.[35]

Beans, Peas, and Legumes

Among the vegetables that Americans ate, none had a stronger association with regional cultures than beans. Baked beans were considered the quintessential New England dish, cooked overnight in a special bean pot, typically with salt pork, and suggesting the frugality associated with Yankee culture. Black-eyed peas were associated with southern cooking and formed a connection between the foodways of Africa and those of the descendants of enslaved people in America. In the Southwest, beans were staples of Mexican American cooking, so much so that "Several observers reported that meals were seldom served without them."[36] Recipes for frijoles and frijoles con queso began to appear in English-language American cookbooks around the end of the 19th century. Refried beans were a dish especially associated with the American Southwest and borderlands. Pinto beans were boiled and then mashed and fried in lard.

Beans of all kinds were used commonly in soups in all parts of the country. Legumes that were eaten without their pods, such as kidney beans, navy beans, and green peas, were typically cooked for long periods, although as new technologies entered the kitchen, cooking time declined. In 1991, one Kentucky man remembered his mother's way of cooking beans, which was "better than pinto beans that you have now that you try to put in the pressure cooker and get ready in twenty minutes." During his youth, in the 1930s, he recalled, "you get 'em started cooking, and you scoot 'em back on that old wood-stove, and just let 'em cook slow." His mother would "cut off a chunk of bacon, side bacon, and then cut it down . . . and that's the way she seasoned her beans."[37]

Green peas cooked with butter were sometimes served as a side dish. When cooked this way, they were generally identified with French cuisine. Cookbooks often suggested green peas as a garnish to roast lamb. Home cooks usually used dried legumes when preparing soups. During the 20th century, however, more and more recipes referred to canned green peas, although dried peas were still called for in making pea soup. Green beans, which were always cooked in their pods, were treated like other green vegetables, usually boiled for some time and served in white sauce.

Beginning at the turn of the century, cookbooks and recipe pages of local newspapers regularly included recipes for "meatless" meals. In such meals, beans featured prominently as providing replacement for the protein in meat. This change did not reflect any significant movement toward vegetarianism, but rather a new interest in nutrition and, during the Great Depression, a real need to economize. Lentils often turned up in these recipes as a particularly satisfying stand-in for meat. A 1910 newspaper column declared: "Lentil as a food has been too long neglected in America."[38] Lentils were common in French and English foodways, this writer noted, but not yet fully adopted by Americans.

Lentil Cutlets

Take a teacup of Egyptian lentils, boil them in water sufficient to cover them until tender. Add three grated onions, some chopped parsley and thyme, and enough bread crumbs to make a stiff mixture. Turn on two large plates and flatten with a knife. Then cut into light triangular sections and shape them like small cutlets. When cold, fry crisp in egg and bread crumbs after inserting small pieces of macaroni into each pointed end. Serve with mint sauce or tomato sauce.[39]

For Asian Americans, who primarily lived on the Pacific Coast, tofu, a soybean product, was an important part of the diet. Many families made their own tofu, but it was also available commercially as early as 1875. Americans of European ancestry did not think of soybeans as food for humans, raising them instead for livestock feed. A 1907 article in the *New York Tribune* described tofu as the "bean cheese of the orient" and explained how it was made and its importance in Asian cuisine, but did not offer recipes for cooking it.[40] The *Chinese-Japanese*

Cookbook of 1914 explained to non-Asian readers: "Tofu is made from a mixture of soyu bean and rice. It is mashed and rolled into a thin cake, and fried in oil, very much like pancakes."[41] During the food shortages of the Great Depression, nutritionists who worked for the U.S. Bureau of Home Economics attempted to convince non-Asian Americans to incorporate soybeans into their regular foodways. A 1934 bulletin produced by the U.S. Department of Agriculture explained: "Forage crops are intended as food for livestock. But some forage crops furnish excellent food for human beings, and this fact now has a new importance in the drought-stricken Middle West." In "the orient," people had for centuries used "soybeans largely for their own food, in place of meat and dairy products." Americans could do it, too, and without changing their cuisine at all. Soybeans should be prepared in the same way that European Americans typically prepared lima beans or green peas, "boiled and seasoned with butter or salt pork; or creamed; or in succotash; or scalloped with tomatoes, corn, and breadcrumbs." If feeling adventurous, an American cook might try "An oriental way to serve soybeans" and simply boil the beans in their pods in salted water, and then eat them straight from the shell.[42] And lest anyone worry that by eating what would otherwise be forage, or livestock food, they would starve a cow, the bulletin assured readers that humans would consume only a tiny fraction of the soybeans grown.

Although Americans had been eating peanuts, also known as ground peas or goober peas, since before the American Revolution, it wasn't until the beginning of the 20th century that peanuts became profitable agriculturally. Harvesting machinery produced peanuts for the market that were stripped of stems, making them easier to package and sell. George Washington Carver, the great American botanist, focused much attention on peanut cultivation, advocating the planting of peanuts as a commercial crop. Around the turn of the century, peanut butter or peanut paste began to be recommended as a health food. Peanuts were suggested by many cookbooks as fillings for sandwiches. Recipes typically directed the reader to make her or his own peanut butter. One recipe from 1905 instructed the reader to boil peanuts and then mash them with butter and salt before spreading on bread.[43] Another, from 1914, used freshly roasted peanuts, which were to be pounded in a mortar and mixed with thick cream. The resulting paste was to be spread on bread and topped with shredded lettuce.[44] By 1920, peanut butter was available commercially, although, as one writer explained, "on account of the high fat content" peanut and nut butters "are apt to become rancid so are usually marketed in small jars."[45]

FRUITS

As well as forming the basis for salads, fresh fruit was commonly used in a few favorite pies—apple, cherry, and peach—and for preserves, which most cookbook writers until the 1920s assumed women would make for their families. At the same time that recipes for fruit preserves began to disappear in the popular food press, it also became less common to find instructions for pickling and preserving vegetables. Increasingly, Americans could expect to buy mass-produced preserved fruits and vegetables from grocery stores. In the 1930s, when the Great Depression shrank family incomes, government workers had to mount a vigorous campaign to remind American women how to make the fruit and vegetable conserves that could save their families from a winter of malnutrition. During this same period, some destitute men, women, and children were able to earn money by selling fresh apples on street corners in cities. The depression coincided with several years of surplus apple crops, which farmers sold cheaply to the unemployed who then resold them to urban consumers.

Fruit salads were served with savory dressings and played the same role as vegetable salads, as appetizers or lunch dishes rather than desserts.

With some notable exceptions, the fruits that Americans consumed grew abundantly in their own country. Apples and pears were most popular. Favorite stone-fruits, as reflected in cookbooks, were peaches, cherries, and apricots. Strawberries, raspberries, and blackberries appeared frequently in preserves and pies as well, with blueberries, cranberries, and loganberries more regional favorites. Among the citrus fruits that grew in Florida and California, oranges were by far the most popular, although by 1940, it was noted that "papayas, mangoes, and guavas" from Florida "are now sold in increasing quantities in New York City." Interestingly, they were not exclusively sold as luxuries; good prices could be found "if one sidesteps the specialty shops" and goes to a market "patronized by South Americans, West Indians, and Mexicans."[46] Pineapple was easily the most popular imported fruit, probably because canning made it so easy to store and use. After 1903, when James Dole discovered how to can pineapple, the fruit rapidly became part of mainstream American foodways and a very popular ingredient in salads. A 1909 advertisement for canned pineapple described it as "the basis of many elegant desserts."[47]

Bananas gained in popularity during the first years of the 20th century, but in 1896, they were still new enough to justify an article in *Scientific American* about how to peel them. In 1914, cookbook author Martha McCulloch Williams could still lament, "bananas are far too unfamiliar in the kitchen."[48] Americans of northern European ancestry were eating bananas but had not incorporated them fully into cuisine as had Caribbean Americans. To a great extent this remains true today, with banana bread the main exception. When most Americans cook with bananas, they use them for sweet, rather than savory dishes. Fannie Farmer recommended that once a banana was peeled, readers should "scrape to remove the astringent principle which lies close to the skin," then serve slices sprinkled with sugar and lemon juice.[49] Other recipe writers most often put bananas to use in fruit salads, especially those that involved gelatin, presumably because setting the fruit in this way prevented it from browning.

Strawberries were not grown commercially with much success until the 1890s. In this decade, ice-making plants were established in southern states, making it possible for these delicate fruits to be shipped to regions of the country where they did not grow as well. By the late 1930s, the strawberry industry of the Gulf states had progressed so far that "strawberries picked on Monday" in Louisiana "could be on Chicago breakfast tables on Wednesday and Montreal tables on Thursday." Perhaps still in awe of this process, Americans tended to eat their strawberries raw, seldom incorporating them into cooked baked goods.[50]

STARCHES

Between 1918 and 1935, consumption of store-bought baked goods, including bread, increased by 40 percent in the United States.[51] Sales of mass-produced bread grew especially after 1928, when the Chillicothe Baking Company of Missouri first successfully used a slicing machine. The most famous of all packaged bread—Wonder Bread—first gained a national market in the 1920s. By 1939, 85 percent of bread that Americans consumed was produced by 28,000 commercial bakers.[52]

Clearly expressing self-interest, an industry journal, *Baking Technology* announced, "The fact is that mother doesn't do much bread baking any more. She buys it ready made like she does her clothing. . . . The situation does not provoke us to tears." Homemade bread was all very well when it was good, the article argued, but "it lacked uniformity of quality." Uniformity was the gift that mass-produced bread had to offer.[53]

The market in packaged bread corresponded to a new interest in sandwiches, which seems to have peaked in the 1940s. During World War II, Americans who joined the domestic war effort found themselves with brown bags or lunch boxes to fill every day. Cookbooks offered a great variety of fillings, typically dividing them into sweet and savory categories. One author categorized fillings by gender, suggesting that some were appropriate for men and others for women. "Male" sandwiches were those with red meat, whereas women were assumed to enjoy lighter fare and to prefer sweet to savory fillings.

Cookbooks reflect the growing dependence on store-bought bread, offering few recipes for how to make yeast bread. If cookbooks are a good guide, home cooks continued to make biscuits, rolls, muffins, and "quick breads" (which use eggs for leavening) in their own kitchens but bought yeast breads from grocers or bakers. These store-bought breads were almost always made from flour that had been bleached, a process that produced a lighter loaf but also stripped the grain of important nutrients. White flour, because it involved processing, had once been more expensive and therefore associated with the economic elite. The poor and immigrant classes were traditionally identified as eaters of dark dense breads, so when white bread became more widely affordable (thanks to technological advances in flour milling, production, and packaging), its popularity was assured among those who wanted to eat like the rich. In addition to using bleached flour, the new processed breads included milk and more sugar than home cooks traditionally used, changing the nutritional impact of bread in the diet. In 1941, the National Research Council Committee on Food and Nutrition and the Food and Drug Administration collaborated with flour millers to introduce "enriched" flour to the American consumer. This new flour, which would quickly become standard for use by home bakers and commercial bread makers alike, restored thiamin, nicotinic acid, and iron, all of which were lost through modern processing.[54]

Mexican American women typically continued to make tortillas at home using corn meal and to serve these as the family's main breadstuff rather than to buy packaged white bread. By the 1930s, however, most were buying their cornmeal already ground and packaged rather than grinding it themselves as was the custom in Mexico.[55]

When World War II made white flour scarce, a cookbook author suggested that her readers borrow a method from "our pioneer great grandmothers" who also suffered from flour shortages "starting in November and lasting all winter," and replace bread with "the

New Mexican woman preparing tortillas, the flat corn meal bread that was served at most meals in Mexican American homes, 1939. (Courtesy of Library of Congress.)

buckwheat pancake, a good inexpensive he-man food."[56] If this did not appeal she supplied a recipe for soy flour bread.

Grains and Cereals

The most commonly consumed grains in the United States, since the earliest days of European settlement, have been wheat and corn. Corn was native to the Americas and wheat was one of the English settlers' first imports as they attempted to recreate the foodways of their homeland. Wheat has primarily been consumed in the form of flour, used to make bread, biscuits, and assorted pies, pastries, and cakes. Between 1890 and 1945, Americans became more likely to eat corn in its kernel form and somewhat less likely to eat it as corn meal baked in a quick bread—one not requiring yeast for leavening. Corn was one of the first vegetables to be sold successfully in cans and also was easily grown in family gardens. When grown at home, corn might be eaten on the cob or the kernels scraped to make corn fritters, sometimes called corn oysters. Among Americans of Mexican ancestry, dried corn was used to make tortillas and also as *pozole*, used in stews. In the Southeast, grits made from dried corn were a common breakfast dish and cornbread, especially for the poor, remained a staple. A Kentucky woman remembering her youth in the 1930s described a version of cornbread called "Grit Bread," patties made with grated dried corn and water that were either baked or fried. She explained that her mother "would use that sometimes as a touch-up for something that she had left over for lunch. As a bread, see. Rather than havin' to go make biscuits or light the oven."[57] In the Northeast and West, the increasing availability of sliced wheat bread is probably the reason that fewer Americans enjoyed cornbread, in its many forms, as part of their daily meals.

Buckwheat, which had been commonly used in the 19th century to make fried cakes from a yeast dough—something like Russian blinis—became much less used in the 20th century. This change, as with cornbread, was probably a result of the introduction of packaged and sliced wheat breads and the decline of home baking. A late 19th-century fad for breads, muffins, and a kind of breakfast cake called "gems" made with Graham flour, named for the food reformer Sylvester Graham, faded in the early 20th century. Graham flour was a combination of whole wheat and white flour and wheat bran. Other grains had particular uses that did not change over time. For example, barley was used in meat-broth vegetable soups. Oats were used to make porridge and especially recommended for invalids. In the 20th century, oats also appeared in recipes for cookies and breads. Among Eastern European immigrant communities, grains like barley and buckwheat were used as stuffings for dishes such as stuffed cabbage or knishes.

In 1918, the U.S. Department of Agriculture issued a bulletin urging Americans to eat more rice. Compared with all other peoples of the world, even the British, with whom they otherwise had so much in common culinarily, Americans ate a notably small amount of this grain. Per capita consumption of rice for Americans was only six pounds per year, while the British consumed 27 pounds and Chinese and Japanese people ate more than 100 pounds of rice per capita per year.[58] Written in wartime, the U.S. Department of Agriculture bulletin encouraged readers to use more rice to save wheat for export to America's European allies. Recipe columns after the war simply suggested rice as a cheap nutritious way to vary the American diet. Neither motive produced the desired effect as American consumption of rice remained low until after World War II. In the 1930s, a British food chemist, Erich Huzenlaub, introduced a process for polishing rice that did not strip the grain of its nutrients. The process, which involved parboiling, speeded up the time needed to prepare rice. This led to the introduction of "minute" rices, which helped to increase the popularity of this grain in the American market.

For most Americans outside of the South, rice appeared in very few dishes. Rice pudding was the most popular use for rice. As an advertisement for Bursley's Rice lamented, "Too many of my friends think of rice as a dessert. They make delicious puddings and custards with rice but that is as far as they go." Those who went a little further used rice in timbales or croquettes and occasionally added cooked rice to muffins, pancakes, and waffles. Some cookbooks recommended rice milk—made by boiling rice in milk and then pressing it through a sieve—as a good food for invalids. In the southern states, one advertisement for a collection of rice-based recipes claimed, "rice is eaten as an all-the-year-around and every-day-in-the-year vegetable." Rice was especially associated with the cuisine of the South, where it served as the base for the regional Louisiana specialty jambalaya, as well as being commonly served cooked with beans. One recipe writer suggested livening up the old favorite in a surprising way. "Rice in lovely delicate colors is the latest idea to hit our tables," the anonymous writer claimed, "and a bright idea it is too!"[59]

Although potatoes remained central to American foodways, cookbooks also began to include pasta recipes, especially after the 1920s. In 1910, spaghetti was still so unfamiliar to most Americans that an enterprising restaurateur in Chicago offered lessons in a private room for those who wanted to learn to eat it gracefully.[60] By 1912, a grocery in Los Angeles was offering patrons six different brands of macaroni, spaghetti, vermicelli, and alphabet pasta.[61] Pasta recipes in American cookbooks might not have been recognizable to Italian cooks, but nonetheless do represent the opening up of the mainstream American diet to new cultural influences. Pasta was typically used to create casserole-like dishes. Marion Harris Neil's *Favorite Recipes Cook Book,* published in 1931, included an entire chapter on macaroni and spaghetti, suggesting that pasta had become a normal part of American cuisine.[62] Among the choice recipes offered were fried noodles and sauerkraut, which reflected a lack of distinction between the dumpling-like egg noodles of Northern Europe and the smoother and more various pastas of Italy. A "Macaroni Contest" staged by a Massachusetts newspaper in 1935 inspired such entries as "Spaghetti Loaf," "Macaroni Fluff," and the first-prize winning "Italian Delight:"

By 1942, Italian food, or at least an American version of Italian food, had
become almost mainstream. Warren McArthur plant employees enjoy spaghetti
and wine at Tony's Bantam Inn restaurant in Bantam, Connecticut. (Courtesy
of Library of Congress.)

Cook 2 packages macaroni in boiling salted water until tender. Drain and add
3 onions. 3 sweet green peppers (sliced and fried). 1 pound hamburger (fried).
1 can tomatoes. 1 can corn. 1 can lima beans. 1 cup sliced olives. ½ lb grated
cheese. Season highly and mix well. Bake 3 hours in moderate oven.[63]

DAIRY PRODUCTS

In 1956, a professor of dairy husbandry looked back over the
first half of the 20th century and called the preceding 50 years "the
Golden Era of the dairy industry" in America.[64] From 1905 to 1955,
U.S. milk production more than doubled, from 64 billion to 123
billion pounds per year. At the same time, increased government
regulation of milk production undertaken in the interests of public health increased costs for producers, with the result that fewer
independent dairy farmers were able to compete in the growing
market.

The health benefits of milk, especially for children, had long been realized, but milk still presented a danger to consumers because individual cows could pass on diseases, particularly tuberculosis, in their milk. Pasteurization, which kills bacteria in milk by heating and then cooling it down, became possible commercially in the late 1890s, but many consumers and experts had doubts about the safety of the process. Some worried that pasteurization stripped milk of its nutrients, others that it was a way for unscrupulous merchants to sell stale milk.[65] In 1908, Chicago was the first city to pass a mandatory pasteurization law and other major cities quickly followed. In 1911, only about 10 percent of the milk supply in Boston, Chicago, and New York was pasteurized; by 1916, nearly 90 percent was.[66] Paper milk cartons were introduced in the early 1930s, but many consumers continued to buy or have their milk delivered in glass bottles.

Butter consumption declined somewhat as Americans began to use more margarine. Most first encountered margarine during World War I when its use as a butter substitute was encouraged by local and state food conservation agents. Many subsequently accepted the now questioned belief that margarine is less fattening than butter. Published recipes, however, continued to use large amounts of milk and butter in the preparation of vegetables as well as in the cakes, puddings, "creams," and ice creams that were popular through this era. A cookbook designed to help Americans deal with wartime rationing suggested two different ways of "stretching" a butter ration, the first involved mixing butter with cream, the second mixed softened butter with gelatin.[67]

Butter use in baking and frying was further challenged by the introduction in 1911 of Crisco, which provided cooks with a cheap and neutral-tasting shortening. Where animal fat lards and butter either imparted a flavor to foods made with them or picked up this flavor only to pass it on to the next item fried in the fat, Crisco could boast that it did not transmit any flavors at all. Representatives from Proctor and Gamble, the company that made Crisco, claimed, "the culinary world is revising its entire cook book on account of the advent of Crisco." Rabbi Margolies of New York, "said that the Hebrew Race had been waiting 4,000 years for Crisco." Crisco was seen as a boon to Jewish cooks both because it was kosher and because as a vegetable shortening it could be used with both milk and meat dishes.[68]

Although both the quantity and variety of cheese produced in the United States increased impressively between the turn of the century and World War II, cookbooks did not reflect this change.[69] Most recipes that used cheese referred only to "grated cheese." Occasionally,

Parmesan was specified and one cookbook author claimed that Roquefort salad dressing was "considered the 'best ever' by connoisseurs."[70] Although the per capita consumption of cheese increased from 2.4 pounds in 1909 to 7.7 pounds in 1954, the numbers of cheese factories decreased as production became centralized through the use of refrigerated train cars and trucks.[71]

Eggs remained an important part of the American diet through the end of the 19th century and the first half of the twentieth. As the population shifted into urban areas, Americans were less likely to keep their own chickens, however, so eggs now came from groceries. The invention of the paper egg carton in 1911 by a Canadian newspaper editor made it much easier to transport eggs reliably to markets.

Egg dishes became increasingly acceptable as food to serve to company, although one author cautioned, "Egg dishes should be highly seasoned to be most appetizing. Combining eggs with other foods makes a more tasty dish than eggs alone." Omelets—both sweet and savory—appeared frequently in cookbooks and the recipe sections of magazines and newspapers. In 1930, a recipe columnist noted that "A guava jelly omelet either pleases the family tremendously or they do not like it at all, but it is well worth trying."[72] Orange omelets, like the following recipe, were often recommended as healthy food for convalescents but also suggested as appropriate to serve to lunch guests.

Orange Omelet

Separate the yolks and whites of six eggs. Beat separately. Mix two tablespoonfuls of powdered sugar, one-fourth teaspoonful of salt, one-half teaspoonful of cornstarch, two teaspoonfuls of lemon juice and one half cupful of orange juice. Beat the egg yolks and add to this mixture. Beat the egg whites until stiff and fold in, then turn into a hot, well buttered omelet pan and cook as usual. Serve garnished with sliced oranges sprinkled with sugar.[73]

SWEETS

Writer Nelson Algren, who studied the foodways of Midwestern Americans in the 1930s, testified to the American sweet tooth. At family reunions in Indiana, Algren observed, it was only after many dishes had already been devoured that dessert was brought out and "the cakes are cut—angel food, devil's food, banana, marble, sponge, coconut, orange, burnt sugar, and lazy daisy. These are followed by pumpkin, cherry, apple, mince, peach, blackberry, and custard pies."[74]

His list reads like the index to a dessert chapter out of any one of many contemporary cookbooks. With Algren's evidence one can state that not only did Americans make all of the cakes suggested in these chapters, but sometimes they made them all for one event.

In whichever form seemed most toothsome to them, Americans consumed 2,600,000 tons of sugar by 1900 and the amount continued to grow.[75] Average per capita sugar consumption between 1891 and 1895 was almost 65 pounds; by 1911 to 1915, it was just over 86 pounds.[76] As a result of the Spanish-American War, sugar companies in Cuba, Puerto Rico, Hawaii, and the Philippines were able to export sugar to the United States either without paying import taxes at all or paying very low rates. The companies that profited from this arrangement were owned and run by Americans.

As well as making cakes, pies, and cookies, home cooks also made a variety of candies. Candy making was often a social event for young women. From the 1890s through the 1920s, the numbers of women who attended college continued to rise, bringing together in dormitories and sorority houses many young women who were the first in their family's history to leave home before marriage and the first to live with large numbers of their peers in semisupervised arrangements. Fudge making and taffy "pulls" served as study breaks. In one popular novel, published in 1912, a college student describes a typical Friday evening in her dormitory: "Six friends dropped in to make fudge and one of them dropped the fudge—while it was still liquid—right in the middle of our best rug."[77]

Other kinds of candy made at home and included in cookbooks through the 1940s were nut brittles, divinity, penoche, butterscotch, caramels, marshmallows, fondants, and nougat. One recipe book, *When Mother Lets Us Make Candy*, published in 1915, borrowed the new language of nutrition to claim that "wholesome candy in limited quantity at proper times has an acknowledged food value."[78] Another cookbook writer warned readers away from store-bought candy. Not only was it bad for one's "figure, complexion and teeth," but "Another, even more dangerous feature of 'Store' candy is the poisonous coloring and dye used." Readers were urged to "never eat these highly colored candies" and to make fudge at home instead.[79]

During the Great Depression, sugar consumption declined when it became difficult for many families to afford necessities. Depression-era recipe writers suggested using dried fruits, honey, and molasses to satisfy cravings for sweetness. Following this advice, Eleanor Roosevelt, wife of President Franklin D. Roosevelt, served stewed prunes for dessert at the White House as part of her attempt to set an example of budget living for the millions of Americans in straightened circumstances.[80]

When America entered World War II, rationing limited the amount of sugar each family could buy, leading to renewed interest in substitutions. A 1942 cookbook designed for wartime living offered a chapter on sugar substitutions, providing general instructions for how to use honey, molasses, maple syrup, or corn syrup in place of sugar. Molasses might make a cake denser, the author informed her readers, but at least it would have the effect of keeping it from drying out.[81] This would be a particularly good thing if, as the author suggested, you sent the cake overseas as a gift for a soldier. Wartime recipes like these reflected the importance of dessert in American foodways when they provided techniques to continue making and eating sweets at a time when it might have been easier to simply cut these out of the diet. A cookbook from 1940 offered readers a simple recipe for war shortbread that included limited amounts of butter and sugar, two rare commodities. A recipe for rolled honey nut cookies managed to avoid using butter and sugar altogether by substituting margarine and molasses.

War Shortbread

8 ounces H.O. quick oats. 4 ounces butter. 4 ounces sugar. Mix above ingredients in a bowl. Put flat onto a board. Cut in squares. Bake at 300° F. for ten minutes; increase heat to 350° F., and bake another ten minutes.[82]

When not experiencing shortages of sugar, Americans seem to have continued to enjoy the kinds of layer cakes described by Algren. These were typically frosted with butter cream or boiled frostings. Fruitcakes were also popular, particularly as wedding cakes, and a wide variety of puddings, "creams" and russes seem to have maintained popularity as cakes became somewhat less common later in the century. Puddings were typically steamed, using a method that had a long history in English cuisine but that is seldom practiced in the 21st century. A cream was made either as a flavored custard or as flavored whipped cream. Russes were more elaborate, using gelatin, whipped cream, and whipped egg whites to achieve an ethereal texture and often also including wafers as a base.

Improvement in transportation and production also made it possible for the owners of ice cream factories to meet Americans' demand for their product. The first use of the ice cream cone is still debated by historians, but it is clear that cones became widely available after the turn of the century and that, by the 1920s, iced desserts served on sticks were popular with consumers. In 1923, Harry Burt patented the process of serving chocolate-coated ice cream on a stick and then began selling what he called the Good Humor bar from trucks. The simplicity of his white truck and the uniformity of the product appealed to a new interest in sanitary food practices that emerged in the early 20th century. Similar chocolate and ice cream treats invented in the same era were the Eskimo Pie and the Klondike Bar.

In 1906, per capita ice cream consumption was almost one gallon; by 1946, consumption had reached a peak of five gallons per person per year.[83] Soda fountains began serving ice cream "sundaes" in the 1890s. Although the origins of the dish and its name are disputed, the basic ingredients—ice cream and chocolate syrup—were both staples of the soda fountains that were popular gathering places for the first 50 years of the 20th century. The addition of bananas to the sundae in 1904, reportedly the idea of a soda fountain manager in Latrobe, Pennsylvania, resulted in another classic American treat, the banana split. Cookbooks included recipes for a range of ice cream flavors that is less familiar now, including burnt almond, macaroon, caramel, grape nuts, and ginger. A cookbook that purported to reveal the specialties of each state included avocado ice cream as representative of New Mexico, and brown bread ice cream as a Massachusetts specialty.[84] The authors also noted that "a lady who had a nice little eating place in Reno conceived the idea of performing a metamorphosis of 'Rocky Road' candy into 'Rocky Road' ice cream" resulting in a flavor that is still popular today.[85]

BEVERAGES

The American love of coffee, which grew through the 19th century, resulted in many strongly held beliefs about how this beverage should best be prepared. Fannie Farmer assured her readers that "Fatigue of body and mind are much lessened by moderate use of coffee," and gave the beverage almost heroic properties when she claimed "severe exposure to cold can better be endured by the coffee drinker." Warning that coffee could be too stimulating, however, she urged her readers to drink it in moderation. Like many of her contemporaries, Farmer believed that coffee beans should be bought fresh in small quantities and both roasted and ground at home. Most cookbooks advocated roasting the beans in a frying pan. Small quantities were important because coffee could easily stale. For this reason, one author suggested that if the coffee was to be kept "in the house any length of time it is best to buy it roasted and grind it in a coffee mill as needed for use."[86]

Among the ways to prepare coffee, the filtered method was identified with the French and the boiled method "preferred" and "more economical" according to Farmer. The method used by one character in a popular book series was representative of the norm during the 1920s: "Tony . . . knew how to be useful, mixing an egg with the coffee, filling the pot with cold water, and setting it to boil."[87] For many Americans until the 1950s, when electric percolators became common, making coffee involved not just coffee and water but also an egg, complete with shell. According to common wisdom, "coffee is much clearer made with egg" as grounds clung to the shell and so could be more easily separated from the liquid.[88] Fannie Farmer also claimed that coffee made with an egg "has a rich flavor," and thus that only dire poverty should prevent one from using this method. Other recipes placed coffee grounds in a flannel bag to be steeped in hot water or milk, and there was much debate about whether boiling the grounds in the water or steeping them in already boiled water was the better method.

Rationing in World War II made coffee a rare commodity. Some advocated stretching beans with chicory, a traditional Louisiana practice or with Figco, or Soyfee, two commercially produced substitutes. One cookbook identified "cereal coffee" as particularly belonging to Kansas. To make it, readers were instructed to roast a pound of barley, a half pound each of wheat and corn, a quarter pound of chicory, "and steep same as any coffee."[89] The same book suggested that one could make coffee "in the form of roasted horse beans as sharecroppers do down south where there's seldom money for the real thing."[90] When using substitutes, if mixed in equal parts with real coffee, "the finished beverage is very acceptable."[91] Others argued that coffee should never be adulterated in this way because coffee "immediately contributes to that gentle lift which leaves no let-down—a lift which only coffee can give."[92]

While Americans also drank tea, it was not as strongly associated with the national character as was coffee. Tea consumption was made more convenient after 1903, when the tea bag was patented. Rather than making a whole pot, consumers could now easily make small quantities and, just as important, steep the drink to individual preference, reflecting tea's role as something most often drunk alone rather than served, as coffee often was, to a larger crowd of guests. As more Americans were able to make ice at home in refrigerators, iced tea, sometimes referred to as "Russian tea," became more popular. Southerners tended to brew their tea with sugar; northerners preferred to serve it "black," leaving the question of sweetening up to the individual. This regional distinction in iced tea preparation has remained to the present day.

Although bottled soft drinks as well as bottled beer had been available since early in the 19th century, a glass-blowing machine patented in 1899 made the mass production of soda bottles cheaper. The invention of "hom-paks," precursor to today's six packs, and the creation of vending machines in the 1920s brought more sodas to more people. Joining the already popular Coca Cola, Pepsi, and Dr Pepper, 7-Up debuted in 1929. Despite Prohibition, which theoretically outlawed getting drunk, 7-Up was marketed as a hangover cure. 7-Up's popularity spread quickly because it was found to be useful as a mixer for the cocktails that became popular during prohibition.

Americans did not regularly consume fruit juice until the 1920s, when orange juice became particularly popular. When they did, it was likely to come from a can. Those who lived in apple-growing regions might drink cider seasonally, but otherwise fruit was typically enjoyed whole. A surplus orange crop in California in the 1910s coincided with the introduction of pasteurization and trucking to make possible the packaging and sale of orange juice to large markets. New canning methods also brought tomato juice and prune juice into American homes. The propagation of information about vitamins and nutrition in the 1920s gave orange juice producers such as Sunkist "just what [they] wanted—a new and mysterious presence in its product about which it could educate the public."[93] Sunkist claimed that, because it had vitamin C, orange juice, could prevent or cure "pneumonia, flu, or common colds." For Americans who had lived through the trauma of the 1918 Influenza epidemic, this gave the juice special appeal. Citrus growers themselves noticed how positively the epidemic had affected sales, as orange juice was one of the few things that the sick were able to consume.[94]

When the Eighteenth Amendment to the U.S. Constitution went into effect in 1920, Americans could no longer legally make, buy, sell, or consume alcohol. There were some exceptions to the rule, as Christian clergy and members of Jewish congregations were allowed to purchase wine for religious ceremonies and doctors could prescribe alcohol to patients. Because these markets continued to exist and the rules were manipulated by devious consumers, some vintners and distilleries were able to remain open. Although alcohol consumption declined during the first year of prohibition, it quickly rose again to near preamendment levels as erstwhile Christians suddenly converted to Jewish rites and as "patients" filled their doctors' orders for Canadian whiskey.

For vintners in California, who had always been overshadowed by European rivals, Prohibition offered an opportunity to take control of the market. Although they could not legally sell wine except to clergy, these clever businessmen found a way to supply other customers. "Bricks of Bacchus," blocks of compressed wine grapes, were sold with packages of yeast and instructions on what *not* to do if the consumer wanted to avoid ending up with wine.[95]

American wine consumption actually increased during Prohibition as consumers carefully failed to follow the warnings on their "bricks," as well as making their own traditional wines from local plants such as dandelion and elderflowers. Many also turned to the more combustible business of home brewing hard liquor, producing "bathtub" gin and grain alcohol. Mainstream cookbooks actually ignored Prohibition and continued to print recipes that included alcohol, such as the several varieties of punches that appeared in Marion Neil Harris's 1931 *Favorite Recipes.*

Breweries were permitted to produce "near beer," which was beer that had been heated so that the alcohol boiled off and contained no more alcohol than one-half of 1 percent by volume. Many simply "failed" to heat their product to the requisite temperatures, whereas others supplied consumers with containers of the alcohol that had boiled off. This was then injected back into the beer, creating what came to be known as "needle beer."

Illegality paradoxically involved many more people in the drinking culture than had participated before. In particular, women, who had risked their reputation if seen entering a public saloon, were able to enjoy cocktails in the semi-privacy of speakeasies and house parties mostly without negative repercussions. In F. Scott Fitzgerald's novel, *The Great Gatsby,* the most famous chronicle of the 1920s, alcohol plays a central role in all social events, as at one of many parties where "the bar is in full swing, and floating rounds of cocktails permeate the garden outside, until the air is alive with chatter and laughter." The title character is rumored to be a bootlegger, or supplier of illegal alcohol, and his reputation does not suffer for the suggestion.[96]

When Prohibition was repealed in 1933 by the Twenty-first Amendment, American drinkers returned to full-strength beer and legal liquor with gusto. Cora, Rose, and Bob Brown, who studied American

A crowd gathers as kegs of beer are unloaded in front of a restaurant on Broadway in New York City, the morning of April 7, 1933, when low-alcohol beer is legalized again. (AP Photo.)

regional cuisines noted that in the seven years after repeal, "so many wine producers have sprung up . . . and there's been so little time to develop fine American vintages that it's hard to know which is best."[97]

Although the Browns wholeheartedly recommended two vineyards in particular, American winemakers tended to focus on the lowest quality products, leaving those who had developed a taste for wine to buy from European markets. By 1940, one cookbook author could complain of a tendency to serve wine "simply to show off." Wine, she argued, ought to be chosen to enhance the food being served. Or, if the wine was really good, the food should be chosen to complement it, reflecting the availability in American markets of some of Europe's finest wines. Wine appreciation should even overcome political commitments: writing just after World War II had begun, this cookbook author declared: "War or no war, the trout cries aloud for a sharp Rhine or Moselle wine."[98]

Two women at the Waldorf-Astoria Hotel in New York City, December 5, 1933, enjoy their first legal cocktail party in many years. Because Prohibition had made drinking a private act, more women became involved in social drinking. (AP Photo.)

NOTES

1. Fannie Merritt Farmer, *The Boston Cooking-School Cook Book* (Boston: Little, Brown, and Company, 1896), p. vii.

2. Janet McKenzie Hill, *The American Cook Book* (Boston: The Boston Cooking-School Magazine Co., 1914), preface, np.

3. Norman D. Humphrey, "Some Dietary and Health Practices of Detroit Mexicans," *Journal of American Folklore* 58, no. 229 (1945): 256.

4. David Horowitz, *Putting Meat on the American Table* (Baltimore: Johns Hopkins University Press, 2006), p. 32.

5. Interview with Pauline Fakes, "WPA Slave Narratives, Arkansas Narratives, Vol. 2, Part 2." Federal Writer's Project, United States Work Projects Administration (USWPA), Washington, D.C., 1941, Manuscript Division, Library of Congress.

6. Zora Neale Hurston, *Dust Tracks on a Road: An Autobiography* (New York: Harper Perennial, 1996), p. 12.

7. Farmer, *The Boston Cooking-School Cook Book,* p. 181. Other recipes for beef a la mode omit the lardoons.

8. Linda Deziah Jennings, *Washington Women's Cookbook* (Seattle: The Washington Equal Suffrage Association, 1909), p. 161.

9. "More Beans and Less Meat," *American Food Journal* 8, no. 1 (1913): 9.

10. "Restaurant Keepers Learn What Meat Is," *Stars and Stripes* 1, no. 8 (March 29, 1918): 1.

11. Rufus Estes, *Good Things to Eat* (Chicago: The Author, 1911), p. 26.

12. Farmer, *The Boston Cooking-School Cook Book,* p. 208.

13. Mary Hinman Abel, *Practical, Sanitary and Economic Cooking Adapted to Persons of Moderate and Small Means* (Rochester, NY: American Public Health Association, 1890), p. 27.

14. Arthur P. Davis, "Growing up in the New Negro Renaissance: 1920–1945," *Negro American Literature Forum* 2, no. 3 (Autumn 1968): 56.

15. L. D. McLean Co., Inc. Grocers. San Francisco, CA: L. D. McLean Co., 1909. http://pds.lib.harvard.edu/pds/view/2846395 (Accessed February 27, 2009).

16. Janet McKenzie Hill, *The American Cook Book* (Boston: the Boston Cooking-School Magazine Co., 1914).

17. Marion Harris Neil, *Favorite Recipes Cook Book* (New York: Wiley Book Co., 1931), p. 204.

18. Neil, *Favorite Recipes Cook Book,* p. 206.

19. Lucy G. Allen, *Choice Recipes for Clever Cooks* (Boston: Little, Brown, and Company, 1924), p. 74.

20. Mrs. G. Edgar Hackney, comp., *Dining for Moderns* (New York: Published by and for the Benefit of the New York Exchange for Women's Work, 1940).

21. Cora, Rose, and Bob Brown, *America Cooks: Favorite Recipes from the 48 States* (Garden City, NY: Halcyon House, 1949), p. 33.

22. Neil, *Favorite Recipes Cook Book,* p. 181.

23. Edwin LeFevre, "Mayonnaise Produced Commercially Since 1906 for Growing Trade," *Yearbook, United States Department of Agriculture, 1930* (Washington, D.C.: Government Printing Office, 1930), p. 372.

24. Lucy G. Allen, *Choice Recipes for Clever Cooks* (Boston: Little, Brown, and Company, 1924), p. 111.

25. Allen, *Choice Recipes for Clever Cooks,* p. 120.

26. Duncan Hines, *Adventures in the Art of Good Cooking* (Bowling Green, KY: Adventures in Good Eating, Inc., 1939). Recipe is #50 (no page numbers).

27. Grace E. Dennison, *The American Home Cook Book* (New York: Grosset & Dunlap, 1932), p. 148.

28. Freda De Knight, *A Date with a Dish: A Cook Book of American Negro Recipes* (New York: Hermitage Press, 1948), p. 122.

29. "If You Know How," *Women's Home Companion,* October 1939, p. 56.

30. *Hamilton (Ohio) Daily News,* June 6, 1929, p. 11.

31. *Big Spring (Texas) Daily Herald,* August 1, 1930, p. 5.

32. Andrew Smith, *Pure Ketchup: A History of America's Favorite Condiment* (Columbia: University of South Carolina Press, 1996), p. 86.

33. Advertisement, *The Housewife*, 26, no. 9 (February, 1910): 11.

34. Janet M. Hill, *Salads, Sandwiches and Chafing Dish Dainties* (Boston: Little, Brown, and Company, 1914), p. 195.

35. De Knight, *A Date with a Dish*, p. 230.

36. Andrew Smith, "Tacos, Enchiladas and Refried Beans: The Invention of Mexican-American Cookery." Presented at the Symposium at Oregon State University. http://food.oregonstate.edu/ref/culture/mexico_smith.html (accessed April, 2008).

37. John van Willigen, and Anne van Willigen, *Food and Everyday Life on Kentucky Family Farms* (Lexington: The University of Kentucky Press, 2006), pp. 24–25.

38. *Olewein (Iowa) Daily Register* March 15, 1910, p. 3.

39. *Olewein (Iowa) Daily Register* March 15, 1910, p. 3.

40. Reprinted in July 11, 1907, Northwood, Iowa, Worth County Index, p. 7.

41. Sara Bosse, *Chinese-Japanese Cook Book* (Chicago: Rand McNally, 1914), p. 78.

42. *Market Basket*, September 5, 1934.

43. *The Times Cook Book*, No. 2 (Los Angeles: Times Mirror Co., 1905?), p. 44.

44. Janet Hill, *Salads, Sandwiches, and Chafing Dish Dainties*, p. 125.

45. Hermann T. Vulte, *Food Industries* (Easton, PA: The Chemical Publishing Co., 1920), p. 163.

46. Brown, *America Cooks*, p. 112.

47. Advertisement for Hawaiian Pineapple in *Housewife Magazine*, 26, no. 9 (September, 1909): 21.

48. Martha McCulloch Williams, *Dishes and Beverages of the Old South* (New York, McBride, Nast & Company, 1913), p. 208.

49. Farmer, *The Original Boston Cooking-School Cook Book*, p. 207.

50. Jane M. Porter, "Experiment Stations in the South, 1870 to 1940," *Agricultural History*, 53, no. 1 (January 1979): p. 94.

51. Clair Brown, *American Standards of Living, 1918–1988* (New York: Harper Collins, 1994), p. 112.

52. James A. Tobey, "Baking Technology and National Nutrition," *The Scientific Monthly*, 49, no. 5 (November 1939), p. 465.

53. "Baker's Bread Provokes no Tears," *Texarkana Press*, reprinted in *Baking Technology*, 4, no. 12 (December 1925): 378.

54. "Vitamin-Enriched Flour Goes Into Production," *Science News Letter* (February 8, 1941): 83–84.

55. George Sanchez, *Becoming Mexican-American* (New York: Oxford University Press, 1995), p. 189.

56. Ida Bailey Allen, *Double-Quick Cooking for Part-Time Homemakers* (New York: M. Barrows and Company, 1943), p. 164.

57. van Willigen, *Food and Everyday Life on Kentucky Family Farms, 1920–1950,* p. 21.

58. United States Department of Agriculture Farmers' Bulletin No. 1195 "Rice as Food," 1918.

59. "Rice in All Colors of Rainbow is Taking Our Tables by Story," *Moberly (Missouri) Monitor-Index,* September 6, 1935, p. 5.

60. "How to Tame Spaghetti," *American Food Journal,* 5, no. 8 (August, 1910): 7.

61. H. Jevne Co., *Established 1882: Grocers, Importers, Manufacturers, Bottlers, Jobbers and Retailers.* (Los Angeles, CA: H. Jevne Co., 1912.).

62. Neil, *Favorite Recipes Cook Book,* p. 137.

63. Recipe published in *North Adams (Massachusetts) Transcript,* April 27, 1935, p. 7.

64. John J. Sheuring, "The Nature of the Dairy Enterprise," *Journal of Dairy Science,* 39, no. 6 (1956): 900–902.

65. Harvey Levenstein, *Revolution at the Table* (Berkeley: University of California Press, 2003), pp. 130–31.

66. The Editorial Board of the University Society, *Child Welfare Manual* (New York: The University Society, 1916), p. 185.

67. Allen, *Double-Quick Cooking for Part-Time Homemakers,* p. 182.

68. Marion Harris Neil, *A Calendar of Dinners* (Cincinnati: The Proctor & Gamble Co., 1922), pp. 9, 19.

69. Neil, *A Calendar of Dinners,* p. 901.

70. Lucy G. Allen, *Choice Recipes for Clever Cooks* (Boston: Little, Brown, and Company, 1924), p. 120.

71. Sheuring, "The Nature of the Dairy Enterprise," p. 901.

72. "Household Suggestions," *Kokomo (Indiana) Tribune,* February 28, 1930, p. 25.

73. Nellie Maxwell, "Kitchen Cupboard: Company Dishes," *The Tyrone (Pennsylvania) Daily Herald,* December 12, 1929, p. 5.

74. Nelson Algren, *American Eats* (Iowa City: University of Iowa Press, 1992), p. 37.

75. Roy A. Ballinger, "A History of Sugar Marketing Through 1974," *Agricultural Economic Report* No. AER382, March 1978, p. 8.

76. Ballinger, "A History of Sugar Marketing Through 1974," p. 16.

77. Jean Webster, *Daddy-Long-legs and Dear Enemy* (New York: Penguin Classics, 2004), p. 71.

78. Elizabeth DuBois Bache, *When Mother Lets Us Make Candy* (New York: Moffat, Yard and Co., 1915), p. 13.

79. Mariposa, *The Hollywood Glamour Cook Book* (Miami, FL: Glamour Publications, 1940), p. 237.

80. Mary Meade, "White House Meals in the Economy Class," *The Chicago Daily Tribune,* May 18, 1933, p. 25.

81. Prudence Penny, *Coupon Cookery* (Hollywood, CA: Murray & Gee, Inc., 1943), p. 31.

82. Hackney, *Dining for Moderns,* p. 69.

83. Hackney, *Dining for Moderns,* p. 69.

84. Brown, *America Cooks,* pp. 393, 586.

85. Brown, *America Cooks,* p. 534.

86. Marion Harris Neil, *Favorite Recipes Cook Book,* p. 298.

87. Maude Hart Lovelace, *Betsy and Joe* (New York: Harper Trophy, 1995), p. 195.

88. Marion Gregg, ed., *The American Women's Voluntary Services Cook Book: A Book for Wartime Living* (San Francisco: Recorder Sunset Press, 1942), p. 15.

89. Brown, *American Cooks,* p. 247.

90. Brown, *American Cooks,* p. 421.

91. Penny, *Coupon Cookery,* p. 102.

92. Allen, *Double-Quick Cooking for Part-Time Homemakers,* p. 53.

93. Douglas Cazaux, *Orange Empire: California and the Fruits of Eden* (Berkeley: University of California Press, 2005), p. 110.

94. *Proceedings of the Fifty-sixth Convention of California Fruit Growers and Farmers,* 1924, p. 117.

95. John Kobler, *Ardent Spirits: The Rise and Fall of Prohibition* (New York: Da Capo Press, 1993), p. 240.

96. F. Scott Fitzgerald, *The Great Gatsby* (1925; repr. New York: Scribner, 1999), p. 27.

97. Cora, Rose, and Bob Brown, *America Cooks,* p. 44.

98. Hackney, *Dining for Moderns,* p. 6.

CHAPTER 3
FOOD PREPARATION

Change came rapidly to the kitchens of America through the first 50 years of the 20th century. This was true both for private kitchens and for those of restaurants and commercial food producers. Some of the poor and those who lived in isolated rural areas continued to cook using the same tools and techniques available to their grandparents, but most people who prepared food were able to use the new gas or electric stoves to prepare their food and, after the 1920s, larger and more efficient refrigerators to store their ingredients and their leftovers. Commercial food production was mechanized during this era, making it more and more likely that a simple staple like bread would be bought in a store, never having been touched by human hands until the customer tore open the wrapper. Thus Americans' relationships with their food changed in this era as more products were bought in stores rather than produced at home, and simultaneously more gadgets, such as toasters and chafing dishes, became available for preparing food within the household.

In 1890, an Iowa farm wife wrote that having one's own icehouse and "freezer" improved life noticeably for herself and her family. Instead of "standing over a hot stove baking pie" she could "make a freezer full of cream and have it frozen in half an hour."[1] The freezer that so delighted this woman was a hand-cranked ice cream maker made of wood, and her ice house was a wooden shed lined with sawdust in which the family stored large blocks of ice, either collected by themselves during the winter, or purchased from an ice merchant. Almost 50 years later, in 1937, a cookbook author could remind readers: "Not so many years ago frozen desserts were 'Sunday' fare and reserved for special occasions." She urged them to "Remember when you used to turn the old hand freezer?" and to celebrate with her that "Now with electric mixer attachments, you can let electricity churn the ice cream for you in just a few minutes."[2] And with safe electric refrigerators, available after the 1920s, Americans could keep their frozen treats conveniently in the house.

The American home had been electrified in the intervening years and refrigeration was making major changes in the way ordinary people lived their lives. Electrification did not simply happen overnight, however. It took a concerted effort on the part of electricity suppliers and the federal government to convince Americans that electricity was both safe and useful. Although Americans were quick to adopt electric lighting, it wasn't until 1915 that electricity suppliers saw that by offering wall sockets, they could get consumers to buy household appliances and thus use more electricity.[3] This innovation greatly expanded the market for household appliances, but not by enough to satisfy the electricity suppliers. In 1935, the Edison Electric Institute and the National Electrical Manufacturers Association joined forces "to actively promote kitchen modernization throughout the country."[4] This campaign was complemented by a concurrent push from the Federal Housing Bureau to "modernize" the American kitchen, largely by bringing electricity to homes that did not yet use it. The Bureau "launched an extensive program that included the creation of model modern kitchen displays; radio programs; distribution of modern electric kitchen plan books; a feature motion picture entitled 'The Courage of Kay' in which the subject was dramatized with numerous tie-ins with retailer, appliance and kitchen equipment manufacturers, builders, and others."[5] Agents for these programs encouraged Americans to think that by bringing electric appliances into their homes they were entering a more perfect future somehow ahead of schedule.

REFRIGERATION

As one domestic manual writer declared in 1924, "the electric refrigerator is more than a dream. It is a real fact of accomplishment . . . they prove indispensable in the well ordered home."[6] Although refrigeration was common in middle class homes by the 1870s, the refrigerators of this era were not electrified, requiring large blocks of ice, delivered by ice wagons, to keep foods cold. Large commercial food companies used either electric- or gas-powered refrigeration routinely by the turn of the century, and some companies produced

ice to sell using this technology. It was not until the second decade of
the 20th century, however, that refrigerator models small enough for
household use were developed. These remained expensive and somewhat impractical, costing nearly a quarter of an average American's
annual earnings and needing frequent repair.[7] One of the first models
introduced was the Kelvinator, which went on sale in 1918. Early
gas-powered models used as coolants chemicals such as ammonia that
were toxic and/or flammable, resulting in regular incidents of poisoning and fires related to refrigerators. In the 1920s, models using
Freon gas, which did not present the same dangers, were introduced
and became the industry standard.

Prices of refrigerators dropped through the 1930s as mass production improved, and by the time the United States entered World
War II, about one-half of all American homes had refrigerators. Once
housekeepers could store food in refrigerators, their options opened up

In this refrigerator, photographed between 1920 and 1950,
some food is stored without a cover, and other food is stored in
covered glass boxes made especially for this use. The invention of
Tupperware in 1946 would offer an alternative storage system.
(Courtesy of Library of Congress.)

significantly. Where families had once had to eat the leftovers of lunch for dinner, they could now enjoy more variety in their daily meals.

Electric refrigerators, because they did not need to also store large blocks of ice, could hold larger quantities of food than iceboxes. Freezer compartments allowed families to plan far ahead and to save the bounty of summer for the leaner times of winter without the heavy work of canning and preserving that earlier generations had experienced. Refrigerated train cars and trucks brought fresh produce to markets throughout the country, and canned produce became ever more available, making it less necessary for housekeepers to preserve fruits and vegetables and to store them in their own cellars. Larger spaces also made possible a new type of dessert, the icebox cake. This kind of cake was made by layering sponge cake or delicate cookies such as lady fingers or macaroons with sweetened and flavored whipped cream and leaving the concoction "in the coolest part of the refrigerator for twenty-four hours."[8] The resulting dish had the impressive form of a cake and the cold creaminess of ice cream. During the 1920s and 1930s, it was frequently served to dinner guests as a novel and attractive treat.

Household refrigerators were still so new by the end of the 1920s that the U.S. Bureau of Home Economics undertook a study in their bacteriological laboratory in 1929 to find out how long different kinds of food—particularly milk and meat—could keep at different temperatures. Refrigerator manufacturers and food producers, deeply interested in the outcome of this study, helped to fund it, and the bureau produced a set of six charts to show the importance of proper care and proper refrigeration of food. Inside refrigerators, food had to be stored using covered dishes—either those specially designed by companies like Corning, or those improvised by homemakers—in order to control odors and prevent spoilage. Refrigerator models such as the Coldspot came with their own glass refrigerator dishes for storage. Sears Roebuck sold replacements for this model, as well as enameled tin refrigerator dishes with glass tops. These containers were useful but, when made of glass, they were heavy and breakable. The introduction of Tupperware in 1946 solved both of these problems, providing families with lightweight unbreakable storage containers that sealed food and its odors neatly beneath a "burpable" top.

OVENS

Not only were Americans storing their foods in new ways—fresh and frozen rather than pickled and preserved—they were also using new kinds of stoves to prepare their food. Both gas and electric stoves were introduced to American homes in the 1920s, but gas stoves were by far the more popular. Both types replaced the ubiquitous cast iron stoves of the 19th century and by doing so freed the women who worked in kitchens from the onerous task of hauling fuel to start the stove each morning. Because the source of heat was constant and could be raised and lowered predictably with the turn of a knob, the electric and the gas "range" made kitchen labor noticeably lighter for homemakers. The new ranges became commonplace in American homes by the 1920s, although they remained more expensive than cast iron stoves. Sears Roebuck continued to advertise not only cast iron stoves, but also hybrid stoves that could burn either gas or coal, and stoves that doubled as kitchen heaters, suggesting that many consumers were not ready to make the shift to the new technology, despite its convenience.[9]

Because gas and electric ranges conducted heat to pots and pans more quickly, lighter metals could be used for cooking. This meant that cooks no longer needed to heft heavy cast iron pots and pans onto the stovetop or into the oven. Because the gas and electric ranges were made of lighter material than cast iron stoves, they could be taller, reducing the amount of stooping that a cook would have to do. To those who had been used to the traditional stoves, the new models, which stood high on long legs, might have seemed to be floating in the air. The new stoves were also easier to clean because they had no fuel-burning compartment to fill up with ashes. This technological change occurred in an era when fewer families were hiring household servants and facilitated this decline in the use of kitchen "help" by making it easier and therefore more attractive for the woman "of the house" to do her own kitchen work.

An advertisement in a British cookbook from the era claimed infallibility for the gas range: "If you have a gas cooker in your kitchen and your dinners are not well served, you may justly blame the cook, who has every advantage that science can give."[10] For the woman who did her own cooking, this advertisement might well induce shame. Another advertisement, paid for by the American Gas Association, asked "Isn't it fun to dream about a house where most of the dreary work is done by magic? Well, keep on dreaming . . . for tomorrow many of your wishes are *coming true!*"[11]

The most liberating development in cooking was the self-regulating oven, which used a built-in thermometer to reliably bring the oven's temperature to a required level and keep it there. Previous oven thermometers could let the cook know when a desired temperature was

Americans were eager to acquire electric stoves, but many, as shown here in a 1940 photograph, also kept their coal- and wood-burning ovens for times when electricity was too expensive. (Courtesy of Library of Congress.)

reached, but it was then up to her to maintain this level by continuing to supply fuel. Now recipes could indicate specific degrees and lengths of time for baking items such as breads or meats rather than leaving the cook to work with less precise suggestions such as "bake in a hot oven." Each oven is different, but self-regulation, a feature of both gas and electric ovens, still takes much of the guesswork out of cooking.

Gas and electric stoves were also innovative in that they radiate less heat than iron stoves and so keep both kitchen, and cook, cooler. Making cooking less hot work made it seem more appropriate for middle class women, according to traditional gender and class ideals. This change in kitchen temperature also opened up the kitchen as a place for family socializing rather than purely a workplace. House designs of the 1920s began to include dinettes or breakfast nooks in the kitchen, sometimes supplementing and sometimes replacing the more formal and distinct dining room. This change was a reflection of increasing informality in American family life made possible by the change in kitchen technology. Eating together in the kitchen, families bonded in a more democratic way than their 19th-century forebears arranged by rank in the formal dining room. By the middle of the century, domestic architects were opening up the kitchen to the rest of the house, actually removing the walls that separated it from living space.

Psychologist Abraham Meyerson saw the new ovens as both liberating for housewives and better for men's health:

> We need to break away from traditional cooking apparatus and traditional diet. The installation and use of fireless cookers, self-regulating ovens, is a first step. The discarding of most of the puddings, roasts, fancy dishes that take much time in the preparation and that keep the housewife in the kitchen would not only save the housewife but would also be of great benefit to her husband. The cult of hearty eating, which results in keeping a woman (mistress or maid) in the kitchen for three or more hours that a man may eat for twenty or thirty minutes is folly.

The lighter meals potentially produced with the self-regulating oven were thus both "ethical and healthy."[12]

At least one cook experienced the change in the kitchen as an awkward reality, not a dream-come-true. Cookbook author Freda De Knight referred to "a woman who has been cooking for the fashionable families of Nashville for the last forty years." The family who employed this seasoned professional installed an electric range in their kitchen, along with many other "modern gadgets, to simplify her work in her old age." What the family forgot was that her "old age" represented years of honing technique. "At first she regarded these innovations with some suspicion, but she knew that modern life demanded modern methods." So she carefully adapted her traditional recipes to the new technology, learning, for example, how to steam a pudding without using a traditional method of placing it in a paper bag.[13]

In 1937, etiquette maven Emily Post credited the new technology with enlivening the American woman's interest in "the beauty of her house and table." She argued: "Perhaps the greatest credit of all is due to the inventors of the unending electric devices which have magically reduced the time-taking and muscle-tiring elements of cooking to the mere turning of a switch; and put the uncertainties of a temperamental oven into the efficient keeping of a thermometer and a clock!" Kitchen technology, Post declared, had liberated American women from a life in which they were slaves to their stoves.[14] A 1926 advertisement paid for by a power company showed a picture of a woman teaching her young daughter to play piano. This quality time was made possible, the ad informed readers, by new technology: "Mother has plenty of time to devote to the education of her boys and girls if she has a Reliable Gas Range with . . . Oven Heat Regulator.

She may place her baking or Whole Meal in the oven and be out of the kitchen for hours by merely turning the little Red Wheel to the correct temperature."[15]

Another ad promised that marital bliss could be found only in the home with a self-regulating oven. "Don't let wedded happiness stop after two short weeks," the advertisement warned, relying on traditional notions that a man was only happy with a wife who could cook: "No inexperienced bride need ever fear failure with any of her baking" if she used the advertised brand of self-regulating oven.[16]

At the end of the 19th century and the beginning of the 20th, the fireless cooker briefly became popular among home economists who attempted to convince ordinary women to use it. A fireless cooker consisted of a vertical stack of interlocked cooking vessels. The food in the bottom vessel, usually meat, was first heated on a conventional stove. Then the other vessels were filled with raw ingredients for other dishes and stacked on top of the first one. Heat rose through the chambers throughout the day, producing a fully cooked evening meal that used only a small amount of fuel and required no attention from the housekeeper. Home economists liked the fireless cooker because, "It not only saves time and fuel but keeps the woman from standing over the hot fire, and there are many foods that are better when cooked at a lower temperature."[17]

A reader of the *Housewife Magazine* wrote to her "sisters," the other readers, to testify to the fireless cooker's wonders in 1908. "When I first heard of fireless cookers I was incredulous," she admitted. Her husband, however, convinced her to try the method and she had now been won over. Rather than advocate any particular brand of cooker, she suggested that readers make their own to see if they like the method.[18] Economical as the fireless cooker might be, they were never widely popular, perhaps because they allowed for only one method of cooking, producing similar textures for all of the dishes cooked in them. With a range, a cook might produce in one meal dishes that were fried, baked, steamed, and broiled.

ELECTRIC APPLIANCES

Although electric ranges were never as popular as the gas versions, electric appliances of many other kinds became essential to American kitchens beginning in the 1910s. Among these were the toaster, the coffee percolator, the waffle iron, the mixer, and, during a brief but intense craze, the chafing dish.

The first electric household toaster was introduced in 1910 by Westinghouse. This appliance did not give the user much control over toasting, however, simply heating the bread to one degree of toastedness. In the 1920s, a model with a clocklike device—complete with ticking—was introduced to allow for variations in taste. This was called the Toastmaster and was a great success. It was followed soon after by a silent model that became the industry standard. In 1922, Americans bought 400,000 toasters; by 1950, 4.5 million were sold.[19] No doubt the introduction of sliced bread was partly responsible for this great increase in toasters and toasting.

As with the electric range, advertisements for the toaster claimed that it could enhance marital bliss. A 1908 advertisement for the Vaughn Electric Company urged the reader "Eat Breakfast With Your Wife." In days past, a wife would have had to remain in the kitchen,

In the early 20th century, electric appliances like this chafing dish were plugged into light sockets because baseboard outlets had not yet been added to most homes. (Courtesy of Library of Congress.)

watching her husband's toast either in the oven or in a range-top toaster. But now, The Pacific Electric Toaster "can be attached to any lamp socket and used on your dining table, then your wife may enjoy the morning meal with you and prepare it as it is consumed." The ad dared not go so far as to suggest a man might make his own toast, or, stranger still, make some for his wife.[20] During World War II, military demand for metal meant that fewer household appliances, like toasters, were manufactured. An ad for the Proctor Electric Company that featured a giant toaster surrounded by admiring women declared, "We could sell a million of 'em! . . . if we had 'em!" If a reader was "lucky enough to own a Proctor Pop-up Toaster" the company urged "take good care of it . . . we can't build more until after the war!" Advertising like this helped, the producers hoped, to keep up demand despite the lack of supply.[21]

A short-lived fad of the 1930s was the sandwich toaster, which could also grill small cuts of meat, such as pork chops. Although never anywhere near as popular as the toaster, it does seem to have been revived in recent years with the George Foreman Grill and a national fashion in the early 2000s for pressed sandwiches.

Electric coffee percolators were easily as popular as toasters, providing Americans with a speedier way to prepare their favorite beverage. In general, percolators work by heating water and then allowing it to bubble over and drip through coffee grounds. The first domestic electric percolator was introduced by Landers, Frary, and Clark in 1908. This model boiled water a little at a time, allowing it to "perk" through the grounds more quickly than had earlier percolators. Although some people doubtless still included egg shells with their grounds in electric percolators, a cookbook writer of 1943 suggested: "Make your coffee according to the directions which come with the pot you are using."[22] This implies that most Americans would now be making coffee with the kind of pot—like an electric percolator—that comes with instructions, rather than using traditional boiling methods. The percolator made coffee preparation both faster and easier, a great benefit in an era when speed and convenience were emphasized as the hallmarks of a modern world. It even made a guest appearance in a 1940 song, "Java Jive," in which the singing group the Ink Spots, singing of their love of coffee solemnly intoned "Waiter, waiter, percolator. I love coffee, I love tea, I love the Java Jive and it loves me."

Waffle irons have been in use for many centuries and they were common appliances in American homes before electric versions were introduced, so it was safe for inventors to assume that there would be a market for them. An electric waffle iron was featured with an electric percolator as part of the Edison Electric Appliance Company's Hotpoint Breakfast set, one of its "Hotpoint Servants" offered in the 1920s. Nonelectric waffle irons, heated in a stove, tended to be heavy and required close monitoring, made more difficult by the fact that they could not be opened in the middle of baking. The electric waffle iron, which freed the cook from heavy lifting and hot watchfulness made it possible to have waffles more frequently, thus bringing a treat into everyday life. The toaster waffles of the late 20th century seem to have continued this process. It is perhaps because they have had this reputation for making everyday life special that waffle irons have so often been given as wedding presents.

Electric mixers, which aid in the preparation of cakes and breads, were first developed for the commercial market. In 1904, they were still so new that newspapers in smaller cities and towns regularly reported on their introduction to local bakeries. In 1904, for example, an article in the Coshocton, Ohio *Democratic Standard* announced "Electric Mixer Mixed Dough Fast." Reporting on the installation of a new electric mixer at a local bakery, the article calculated that the bakery could now turn out almost 2,000 loaves of bread an hour, and reassured readers that "at this rate it does not seem likely that the bread supply of the city should run short."[23]

In 1930, the Sunbeam company introduced its Mixmaster, a household mixer that instantly became a commercial success and set the standard for what mixers would look like for the rest of the century. The Mixmaster featured a detachable mixing bowl and a stand that housed an electric motor with which to power a set of interchangeable beaters and paddles. After generations of women had developed strong arm muscles from beating cake batters and kneading dough, the Mixmaster contributed to a major change in the housewife's physique.

Another kind of mixer, also first developed for commercial use, gained popularity in the 1910s and entered the domestic market in the 1920s. These mixers were the early versions of what are now called blenders, although they did not include chopping blades. Mixers of this type were found at soda fountains where they were used to create blended drinks made from combinations of syrups and ice cream, milk, or soda water. Drug stores with soda fountains advertised that they had these mixers, hoping to lure customers from those old-fashioned establishments that still shook their sodas by hand, or stirred them with a spoon. A 1911 advertisement for a drugstore in Marion, Iowa, gives a suggestion of how big a role soda fountain drinks played in the social life of the era. The Carl N. Owens drugstore boasted that its mixer "mixes lemonade, egg lemon shake, egg chocolate, malted milk, egg malted milk, frappe, caramel puff, and all kinds of hot and cold drinks to perfection."[24] It is easy to see how the fashion for frothed up sweet drinks would transform just a few years later into the cocktail craze of the Prohibition era. One soda fountain worker credited the electric mixer with increasing the popularity of chocolate malteds. Before the advent of the mixer, malteds "cost too much, took too much time, and weren't very good when you got them." But once the mixer was introduced, "everybody" wanted them: "Businessmen come in and eat 'em for lunch, the girls soak up hundreds of them every day, and everybody thinks they're just about the last word in flossy drinks."[25] Mixers were so closely associated with the malted craze that in 1928 the Skagg's Safeway grocery in Woodland, California, offered a free mixer with the purchase of a five pound tin of chocolate malted mix.[26] The blender, a close relative of the drink mixer, but with the ability to pulp fruits and crush ice, was invented in 1922 but not "introduced" to the public market until 1937, when it was presented at a restaurant show specifically as a way to mix cocktails. The 1930s were an era of interest in nutrition, so the blender also quickly became popular as a way to create health drinks of various fruit and vegetable ingredients.

With the introduction of electric appliances, the kitchen of 1940 was a very different place from the kitchen of 1900. As early as 1907, a writer suggested how electricity might change human relationships. Where once a man had needed either servants or a wife to feed himself, electricity now gave him true independence. "In the up-to-date cozy apartments of the bachelor of today you will find that electricity to a large extent takes the place of servants" and does the tasks that in married men's houses "is daily accomplished by the touch of dainty feminine hands." With his toaster, percolator, and an electric hot water heater in which to boil an egg, he could start his day quite happily solitary, and for evening entertainments, "With the electric chafing dish half a hundred dainty, nutritious, and appetizing dishes can be easily, quickly, and economically prepared."[27]

The chafing dish experienced a period of intense popularity among middle class Americans between the turn of the century and the late 1920s, provoking the composition of countless recipe books and chapters in cookbooks. Chafing dish popularity preceded the electrification of the home and, like waffle irons, must have seemed like a good bet for electrification. Electric chafing dishes, like electric waffle irons, made it possible to experience more commonly something once saved for special occasions. This may well have led to the decline of the fad. A chafing dish is an ancient form of cookery in which food is prepared in a large broad metal dish over a small heat source. For some dishes, the cooking pan sits in a larger pan of water; for others, it is directly over the flame. Chafing dishes made it possible for cooks to prepare a dish in front of their guests, turning the dinner party into a performance piece. The turn of the century, when Victorian mores were loosening up, was an era in which middle class Americans enjoyed entertaining friends in their own homes, previously a closely guarded private sphere.

The chafing dish allowed the woman of the house to "cook" for friends without disappearing into the kitchen to struggle with pots and pans. Men, too, appear to have taken to chafing dish cookery as a kind of sport, quite unlike typical household cookery in which they were never involved. Perhaps the open flame suggested a manly camp-fire experience. Chafing dish suppers were typically held at midnight, lending them a somewhat risqué air. One cookbook author suggested that eating at midnight might not be good for one's health, but the craze was so pervasive that she nonetheless proceeded to provide a whole chapter of chafing dish recipes.[28]

In 1894, the *New York Times* reported that a group of young women in Brooklyn were taking a course together in chafing dish cookery. These were well-to-do ladies of "the Heights" (Brooklyn Heights, a neighborhood that overlooks the East River and Manhattan) who belonged to some of the clubs that wealthy women of the era joined in large numbers. The activity was not, the article reported, "strictly single-sex:"—"Men were admitted to the evening classes and bankers and brokers vied with their wives in bringing a Welsh rarebit exactly to a turn."[29]

The Welsh rarebit referred to here was far and away the most popular chafing dish recipe, followed by lobster Newburg, which appeared in every chafing dish cookbook and every chapter on chafing dish cookery even into the 1940s. Welsh rarebit (sometimes called "rabbit") was essentially a cheese sauce served on toast. It is a simple dish to make and to eat, somewhat messy, which perhaps recommended it to male cooks who were typically raised to think of themselves as averse to all things delicate. One cookbook author even suggested that it was men who led the chafing dish craze and that women only became involved as part of the larger movement among American women to expand their opportunities in society. Most middle class women had ceded the arts of the kitchen to servants by the turn of the century, but the chafing dish called them back: "By many women cooking is considered, at best, a homely art,—a necessary kind of drudgery . . . But, since women have become anxious to compete with men in any and every walk of life, they, too, are desirous of becoming adept in tossing up an appetizing salad or in stirring a creamy rarebit."[30] As an ode to the chafing dish noted, the wonderful appliance actually replaced the need for and thus the trouble of servants. A happy hostess blithely celebrated the fact that she could exploit the chafing dish in ways no human employee would accept:

> "Ingenious handmaid, well I love
> your smiling copper face, For you never give me notice
> You're going to leave your place.
> . . .

> Your hours are always overtime,
> But no one faints with fright
> Because you're asked to cook for eight
> At twelve o'clock at night!

> You do your hospitable best
> For the slenderest of purses!
> Dear chafing dish, accept these most
> Appreciative verses!"[31]

The chafing dish responded, agreeing cheerfully to its subjugation,

> "I'll never leave you in the lurch
> To seek for higher wages,
> And here's your health, with many thanks

> For mention in these pages."[32]

The cookbook author himself, an English man, suggested that the chafing dish's popularity in America probably stemmed from the "great difficulty experienced there among private families to get qualified cooks."[33]

Although chafing dishes "disappeared from the American home about the time that streamlined kitchen ranges—and efficiency in homemaking—came into being," they experienced a brief revival in the 1940s, explained by one author as reflective of the smallness of modern apartments and a new interest in the aesthetics of the Victorian era. American women, this author argued, still wanted to play the bountiful hostess; they just didn't have any room to do it. A dinner that could be cooked on the table looked like a perfect solution.

Although gadgets like the electric toaster and percolator became more and more common in American kitchens through the first half of the 20th century, it is important to note that they never completely replaced nonelectric kitchen tools. The advent of the electric mixer, for instance, did not cause the disappearance of the hand-cranked eggbeater or the simple whisk, and the 1931 introduction of the electric can opener did not make the nonelectric versions any less popular. In many kitchens electric and nonelectric models of the same tool continue to coexist.

COOKWARE

New technology in appliances was complemented by new developments in cookware. In the 1890s, American manufacturers introduced enameled tinware cooking pots to the market. These pots were much lighter than the traditional cast ironware and could be speckled and even colored to create a more festive looking kitchen. In the late 1920s, the first stainless steel cookware was produced but was mainly used in commercial kitchens. By the 1930s, American home cooks were able to buy stainless steel coated cooking pots with carbon or copper cores. These new pots were light to use and conducted heat much more efficiently than did tinware, giving home cooks more control at just the moment when many were becoming interested in the sauce-based cuisine of France that demanded just such subtlety for its preparation.[34]

At the same time, at least one food writer credited the new interest in European cooking with the revival of the casserole, one of the oldest forms of cookware. Noting that the end of Prohibition brought "a concerted drive in this country to interest women as well as men in wines both domestic and imported."[35] To do this "all phases of gourmet cookery were publicized through the superbly edited decorating and gardening magazines and the smart fashion journals. It was suddenly chic to know how to cook" in the European fashion, which required new cookware as well as new recipes and a new palate.[36] A new interest in casseroles—the meal as well as the dish in which it is cooked—was also a reflection of a changing economy in which more women worked, leaving less time for cooking, and the general trend toward more casual dining. Casseroles fit in well with this trend, as they moved from oven to table and contained a whole meal, obviating the need for elaborate serving dishes. Although casserole cookery may well have been associated with European cookery, it was an American company that, in 1915, brought innovation to the form. In this year, the Corning Glass Company introduced Pyrex, a durable glassware that allowed cooks to observe the baking process, as well as providing a novel way to serve food, as it could go straight from the oven to the tabletop. After World War II, American home cooks' interest in European cuisines grew even more widespread and many homes acquired a whole new *batterie de cuisine* to realize the new fascination.

Another innovation in cookware of the early years of the 20th century was the pressure cooker, which significantly reduces cooking time for any foods that might be prepared in liquid or steamed. Pressure cookers were primarily used in commercial food preparation until World War I. During the war, at a time when the federal government was encouraging Americans to grow and preserve their own food, the U.S. Department of Agriculture issued a bulletin declaring pressure cookers the best method for canning low-acid foods. Although cookers on the market were rather unwieldy, this one bulletin significantly increased the household demand for pressure cookers, which in turn drove the development of a more easy-to-use model that was on the market by the 1930s.

PRESERVATION

The period between 1890 and 1945 saw a decline in the numbers of Americans who grew their own food and therefore a decline in the numbers who preserved part of their agricultural produce for winter months. Many families, however, continued to preserve the fruits and vegetables of their gardens and technological developments assisted them to do so during these years. The most important such development was the patenting, in 1915, of a type of glass jar and lid for preserving that is still in use today.[37] Glass jars had been used since the Civil War era, but had been sealed with wax, a process that was both messy and a little dangerous. The new lids made sealing easier, which led to the increased use of glass jars over metal cans or ceramic jars. A family who canned would use several hundred jars each year. One woman recalled that the houses of her Kentucky community had "a picket fence around the garden [with] fruit jars setting on top of the pickets" because there was not enough storage room in the house for the great number of jars needed to preserve a season's worth of produce.[38] When pressure cookers were made available for home use, they were recommended for canning. Because most women had learned their canning techniques from older female relatives, they were often reluctant to try the new method. State agricultural extension programs sent agents out into communities to teach women how to use the pressure cookers, turning a demonstration into a social occasion in some cases. As one woman remembered, shortly after the end of World War II, a demonstration agent visited and "asked me would I ask all my neighbors in . . . And so I had not a Tupperware party, but a pressure cooker party."[39]

Not only was the pressure cooking method more sanitary than the traditional "open kettle" method, heating jars to temperatures high above boiling, this particular woman and her visitors (who were all inspired to buy pressure cookers) found it "so much faster, so much easier." Even as home canning became safer and easier, it became less essential, as fewer Americans grew food and more processed foods became available through advances in preservation and transportation. In the era of large scale commercial food processing, it could seem willfully old-fashioned to can. For those, like cookbook author Marion Harris Neil, who found that "canning is the best and most desirable method of preparing fruits and vegetables," modern conveniences such as gas and oil stoves made it ever easier.[40] For those who continued to can, storage became a problem. Where houses had once been built with fruit closets, rooms designed to be cool, dry, and dark, new trends in architecture omitted this feature. An agent for the Bureau of Home Economics noted in 1930, "Many small town homes, built for real estate development, lack proper facilities for storing fruits, vegetables, and canned foods in quantities."[41] Cellars could be used, Richmond wrote, but they tended to be too damp. An ordinary closet could be used, but this would mean removing whatever else one might want to store. Architecture and advertising were both working against the tradition of canning food at home.[42]

In the 1930s, some families began to replace or supplement their home canning with home freezing. As the frozen food industry began to expand rapidly through the 1930s, home freezing of meat and produce also expanded. Because not many people had the capacity in their homes to store large amounts of food, community storage facilities opened, in which families could rent space to store frozen food for the winter.[43] This interesting resource disappeared as both freezers and single-family homes grew larger in the years after World War II.

COMMERCIAL FOOD PROCESSING

Although Americans had been buying commercially processed fruits, vegetables, milk, and meats since the mid-19th century, it was difficult for consumers to get reliable information about what was inside the cans they were buying. In 1905, the magazine *Appeal to Reason* published in serial form a novel by Upton Sinclair that revealed some of the unsavory practices of the meat packing industry. In *The Jungle,* Sinclair wrote, "it was the custom . . . whenever meat was so spoiled that it could not be used for anything else, either to can it or else to chop it up into sausage." If meat was "moldy and white . . . it would be dosed with borax and glycerine, and dumped into the hoppers, and made over again for home consumption." Nothing was wasted: "There would be meat that had tumbled out on the floor, in the dirt and sawdust, where the workers had tramped and spit uncounted billions of consumption germs. There would be meat stored in great piles in rooms; and the water from leaky roofs would drip over it, and thousands of rats would race about on it." Workers would kill the rats with poisoned bread, "and then rats, bread, and meat would go into the hoppers together." As Sinclair explained, this is no fairy story and no joke."[44]

Sinclair's work horrified the public and helped reformers who had been urging reforms in the food industry. In 1906, the Pure Food and Drug Act was passed, establishing government inspection of processing plants to prevent the sale of adulterated or mislabeled products, but beyond this basic reassurance, little could be learned about a product from its packaging. Food companies encouraged purchase of their products by providing attractive labeling and advertisements rich with unsubstantiated claims of goodness. No one—neither consumer nor producer—particularly expected to find objective information about the quality of processed foods on labels. This all changed after World War I.

The Warehouse Act, passed by Congress in 1916, made United States Department of Agriculture (USDA) inspectors available to processors of fruit and vegetables who wanted to apply for government loans to expand their warehouses. These government inspectors assigned the processed foods grades from A to C. Corresponding to A, B, and C were the terms *Fancy, Choice,* and *Standard.* It wasn't until the 1920s that consumers began to learn about the grades and their meaning. As one food chemist who worked for the USDA explained, "Their superlative titles and extra prices to the contrary notwithstanding, the Fancy and Choice grades will not satisfy the family appetite any better than the others. In actual food value, the difference between these grades is very slight. The chief distinction is the size and condition of the fruit packed and the strength of the sirup [*sic*] used."[45]

Industry resisted mandatory grade labeling while consumer advocates fought to expand it to all food industries. As shoppers began to read labels, however, producers started to suspect that there might be a benefit to incorporating grade into labeling. The can of peas that did not declare its grade on the label might look like it had something to hide if all the other cans on the shelf proudly declared themselves A, B, or C. A 1940 ad for Del Monte canned foods promised readers, "Del Monte informative labels always tell you what's in the can." The company had adopted the language of the consumer advocacy movement to sell more of its products. Once consumers came to trust this claim, their shopping would, producers hoped, consist of looking for a specific brand, rather than a particular fruit or vegetable, for "one dependable brand covers most of your canned food needs."[46] Ten years earlier, in 1930, a woman who worked at the U.S. Bureau of Home Economics commented on the reliability of labeling: "labels on packages of food products, while still vying with one another to attract the buyer's roving eye, now carry truthful statements as to the nature of the contents, thanks to a strict enforcement of the Federal Food and Drug Act for nearly a quarter of a century. And it is the hard cold facts set forth in these statements—not the appeal to one's sense of the esthetic . . . that permit a sound selection of one out of several cans, cartons, or bottles of any particular product."[47]

Canned foods included vegetables and fruits, both evaporated and condensed milk, various chopped meat products, and condensed soups. Increasingly, recipes included canned ingredients. One 1940 recipe in *Good Housekeeping* magazine was made entirely from canned products, combining a can of mixed vegetables, a can of condensed consommé *Madrilene* (a tomato flavored broth), and a can of condensed tomato soup. Together these would make "a hearty luncheon dish" for the cook "in an adventuresome mood."[48]

To encourage American consumers to turn more often to cans, the National Canners Association sponsored "Canned Foods Week." Retail and wholesale grocers' associations were happy to help out. During the designated week, grocers and other food sellers were encouraged to make displays of their canned foods and to price them in a way that would "induce the consumer to make a thorough test, if this has not been done previously, of all kinds of canned foods now packed for consumption." In particular, the canners stressed the cleanliness of the canning process during which fruit was taken "from the field, and without the touch of human hand prepare[d] for the table of the consumer."[49] Germ theory had only recently been popularized so many food processing businesses used the public's new interest in hygiene to sell their products. The traditional producer, whether butcher, baker, or homemaker, was described as unsanitary and wasteful, whereas industrial processing was praised as flawlessly clean and efficient.

By 1920, the meat processing industry in America had become so centralized and efficient that, one writer reported, a single processing plant could produce many kinds of products: "thus we find the high grades of fat being manufactured into butterine [another name for margarine] in one department, lower grades into soap in another."[50] This author praised the large meat processing plants in comparison to traditional butchers. The plants eliminated waste and imposed higher standards of cleanliness, he argued. In the "sausage department," for example, "the packer finds a way of disposing of those portions of meat that are nutritious but not palatable in their original condition."[51] In the making of sausage, "fillers" such as potatoes, corn flour, and cracker meal were used and spices including "sugar, salt, white or red pepper, cinnamon, mace, allspice, cloves, coriander, caraway seeds, marjoram and onions or garlic" were added for flavor.[52] As well as sausages, "a large variety of meat products is found on the market, some of which have been partially cured, for example corn beef; others contain mixtures of meat, cereal and spices. The latter when finely ground and highly spiced are known as potted or deviled meat."[53] The most famous of these was Spam, introduced to the public in 1937 by the Hormel company and popularized during World War II, when it was included in soldiers' rations.

To get Americans to buy meat in cans, companies had to inspire confidence in the safety of their product. A 1940 advertisement for Armour brand Star Pure Pork Sausage emphasized the idea of cleanliness. To begin with, the product had the word "pure" in its name, a word not generally associated with sausages, which have often been a mixture of meats and spices. Armour's advertisement noted that "Grade A meats" were used to make the sausages and that they were "made fresh every day in kitchens as spotless as your own."[54] In the early 20th century, there was little consumer confidence in the quality of canned meats and they were largely considered low-status food, but as Americans became more and more interested in convenience foods, and the ready-to-eat foods came to be seen as modern, processed meats lost some of their association with poverty. In 1915, meat packing companies began selling bacon in slices. They sold the slices in jars until cellophane was invented in the 1920s. Traditionally bacon had been sold in a large, greasy slab. The new, more elegant-seeming slices enticed wealthier customers to buy; and bacon, which had once been associated exclusively with the poor, became standard fare for all classes. During World War II, meat shortages caused many new customers to turn eagerly to processed meats. The national production of sausages, which require minimal preparation before they can be eaten, tripled between 1904 and 1925.[55]

The need to provide consumers with a product that would not spoil in its can led to much experimentation with preservatives. In many meat packing plants, for example, borax or boracic acid were used as preservatives. Preservative chemicals were frequently used in the early days of commercial food processing, but by 1920, one writer declared, "modern methods of sanitation and sterilization" made them "absolutely unnecessary" for foods that were to be eaten "within a short period."[56] Food processors, however, claimed the chemicals were used in such small amounts that they could not possibly be dangerous. Critics argued that, although not actually poisonous, the chemicals could interfere with proper digestion and also lead packers to use inferior ingredients in their products. For home canners, the loss, through inadequate sterilization, of a batch of canned vegetables could be extremely frustrating, but for the big and growing food processing concerns it could be an economic disaster, for what was lost was not just products but potentially also the public's trust. Preservatives that could limit this risk seemed very attractive.

Much to the dismay of the producers, Harvey W. Wiley, the Chief Chemist of the U.S. Food and Drug Administration, declared Borax unsafe for use in foods and it was banned by the 1906 Pure Food Act. Wiley's study, which involved a mere 12 subjects, all of the same age, health, and ancestry, would probably not be regarded as good science in the 21st century. Wiley found that Borax, although not poisonous, could interfere with natural digestive processes and might damage the kidneys.[57] The Pure Food Act limited acceptable additives to "salt, sugar, wood smoke, vinegar, pure spices, and pending further inquiry, saltpeter."[58] After the act was passed, pork processing companies, eager to speed up the time it took to cure a ham, typically several months, began experimenting with sodium nitrite and nitrate. In the 1920s, a new method by which nitrite was pumped through the veins after butchering made it possible to cure a ham in five days. Taste quality suffered, but faster curing meant more, and thus cheaper, hams.

A home economist writing in 1923 listed, among the many ways that commercial food producers deceived their customers, "harmful preservatives and coloring matter."[59] Processing also included enhancing products through artificial sweetening and/or coloring. Beginning at the end of the 19th century, saccharin was widely used to sweeten commercially processed foods and became especially popular during and after World War I when America experienced sugar

shortages. Food processors used saccharin in the place of sugar because its intense sweetness made it possible to use less and thus save
money. When the Missouri Supreme Court overturned a state law
banning use of saccharine, the Monsanto Chemical Works company,
a maker of saccharine, spelled "saccharin" at the time, celebrated the
news with a full page announcement in the *American Food Journal.*
Saccharine was "much more desirable than sugar," the ad declared,
when it came to sweetening soft drinks because it was both healthful
and cheap. Trading on recent findings that excessive amounts of sugar
were bad for the health, Monsanto deduced that saccharine, because
it was not sugar, was therefore healthy: "In using saccharin the danger
from the use of sugar is eliminated and the infinitesimal amount of
saccharin that is required to sweeten cannot possibly be harmful to
any one."[60]

Artificial coloring was added to make food more visually appealing.
Although coloring helped to sell products, it also worried consumer
advocates who saw that coloring could help producers conceal the true
nature of a product. The 1906 Pure Food and Drug Act that banned
the use of some preservatives also prohibited use of any "poisonous
color or flavor" and made illegal the sale of food "colored, powdered, coated, or stained in a manner whereby damage or inferiority is
concealed."[61] Seven colorings were deemed acceptable, but they could
not be used to delude consumers. During the 19th century, butter
producers had begun to add yellow dye to their product to simulate
the color of butter produced by cows grazed on grass. Traditionally,
the color of butter changed with the seasons as cows ate different kinds
of food. By using coloring, dairy owners could feed their stock on less
expensive hay but make customers think they were getting the highly
valued butter of grass-fed cows. When margarine was introduced, the
dairy industry fought to prevent margarine manufacturers from also
dying their product. Several states even required margarine to be dyed
pink to make clear the fact that it was not butter. The Supreme Court
invalidated these laws in 1898, but margarine makers were still reduced
to selling separate coloring packets with their product until 1950.

In the 1930s, freezing became an economically profitable way to
preserve food for future use. American inventor Clarence Birdseye
first experimented with ways to freeze food quickly in the 1920s. The
faster food freezes, the fewer ice crystals form, preserving the taste of
fresh food. Freezing had the advantage of not requiring any coloring
or preservatives and of maintaining the precise flavor of fresh produce,
rather than adding to it with syrup or brine as canning did. By 1941,
the frozen food industry, which had "had a phenomenal growth" in

the previous 10 years, froze "more than half a billion pounds of many kinds of food a year."[62] The growth of this industry was possible as more Americans acquired refrigerators with freezer compartments. And as food producers offered more and more frozen products—processed foods as well as simple fruits and vegetables—industrial designers made larger freezers to accommodate consumers' growing desire to store their frozen food at home. Neighborhood groceries installed large freezers and advertised on storefront signs that they offered "frozen foods," as a lure to the modern shopper.

As Americans became accustomed to eating fruits, vegetables, milk, and meat from cans or out of freezers, they also became willing to eat cereal out of boxes, bread from sealed packages, and pies that were made by machines. The first 50 years of the 20th century saw the industrialization of the American diet.

Breakfast cereals had become fashionable toward the end of the 19th century, as health advocates like J. H. Kellogg recommended eating whole grains. As the field of nutrition emerged at the beginning of the 20th century, Americans were gradually made aware of the concept of the body as machine, and one that needed "proper" fuel in appropriate quantities and at specific times to function well. Breakfast cereals, made from processed grains and marketed in tidy, sealed paper boxes, seemed to fit this new approach to breakfast. J. H. Kellogg's brother, Will Keith Kellogg, began selling his cornflakes in 1906. Although some of the cereals introduced in the early 20th century are still well known 100 years later, many more, such as Dr. Price's Wheat Flake Celery Food, have since fallen out of fashion.[63]

Writing in 1920, Hermann Vulte identified the four main types of processed cereals on the market: flaked, puffed, shredded, the "variety resembling crumbs," and malted. Flaked cereals, like cornflakes, were produced by flattening out grains that had been heated until they lost all their moisture and popped. Puffed cereals consisted of grains that had been popped but not flattened and followed in an old New England tradition of eating popcorn for breakfast. There was only one kind of shredded cereal—shredded wheat, but Vulte included it in his survey because it was so popular. The process of making it was complicated, involving "some twenty to twenty-five different processes." Cereals "resembling crumbs" included Grape Nuts, which actually *was* bread crumbs, another New England tradition. To make Grape Nuts, wheat and barley flours were mixed, baked into a loaf, sliced, toasted, and crushed.

Although less processed cereals, such as oatmeal, were certainly more economical and the new cereals had no added health benefits,

Vulte did agree that they "are palatable, wholesome, nutritious and variable in flavor. They save much time, labor and fuel in the home," and "From a sanitary standpoint there is an advantage, being sold in cardboard boxes well lined with air-tight paper, they are protected from air, moisture, dust and micro-organisms."

Vulte made similar claims for bread baked and packaged in factories. Thanks to modern technology, "the human hand needs scarcely touch the product from the time that the raw materials enter the building until the finished loaf is ready to be carried out for delivery." In this era there was little interest in artisanal craft among food producers. The human hand was a potential disease carrier, not the tool of genius. As one historian notes, despite the fact that bread wrappings "represented a significant expense, bakers found that the increased sales more than offset it."[64] This was particularly true for crackers, which had traditionally been sold in barrels, with the result that: "The bottom half of the barrel usually contained soggy, broken crackers; and if the cat didn't sleep in the barrel, the mice did."[65] Selling crackers sealed in wax paper envelopes inside paper cartons increased both their price and popularity. Mayor John Mitchel of New York encouraged consumers to save money by buying bulk and rejecting prepackaged goods because "you cannot possibly get as much food for your money when so large a part of your money has to pay for the box, wrapper, printing, etc." Indignant food industry representatives admitted that "certainly, bulk goods may be purchased somewhat cheaper than packaged goods," but "who wants bulk goods, when package goods are within reach?" The reason that packaged goods were superior was "sanitation, wholesome living, clean, uncontaminated whole foods."[66]

By 1918, "About two-fifths of the bread in the United States [was] made in bakeries and three-fifths in the home," as this traditional task of housewives was increasingly outsourced to commercial bakeries. It took some time for professional bakers to mechanize their operations. In 1899, more than 90 percent of bakeries operated without mechanical power.[67] To some extent the desire to stick to traditional methods was probably a point of pride, but it also had to do with distribution. The more bread a bakery could turn out, the more consumers it would have to get that bread to in order to make a profit. As bread is perishable, this would have to be accomplished with great speed.

Those bakers who eventually decided to mechanize production also had to become managers of distribution and marketing, getting their bread into groceries before it went stale. The first big commercial bakers used horse-drawn wagons to move their bread from oven to shelf;

by the 1920s, trucks helped these businessmen distribute their wares farther and faster. Whether one consumed commercial or homemade bread depended largely on what kind of community one lived in. By 1922, a survey of 3,000 families revealed that 94 percent of farm families made their own bread, but only 56 percent of those who lived in cities of more than 25,000 people did so.[68] Commercial baking got a big boost during World War I, when, in order to supply the army and allies, Americans were asked to make two days a week "wheatless," which meant using other types of flour for breadstuffs. With food scientists on staff, it was easier for large bakeries to successfully make the switch to mixed flours than it was for the average housekeeper.[69]

The introduction of sealed packaging for bread made it more appealing to consumers fixated on sanitary goods, and the use of slicing machines made bread suddenly seem like a convenience product. A 1933 ad for "Home Baked Sliced Bread," mass-produced by the

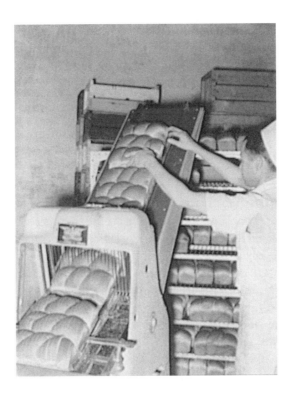

In 1939, the slicing machine at this industrial bakery in Texas turned out uniformly sliced loaves of white bread. (Courtesy of Library of Congress.)

Home Bakery factory, not actually made in a home, announced, "To meet public demand we introduce Home Baked Sliced Bread." Presliced, it was "ready for spread, safe for children, most inviting for the table, most convenient for sandwich, perfect for toaster."[70] Sliced bread saved small children from the danger of trying to use large bread knives, and it kept the table clean of crumbs produced in home slicing. Not only was it cleanly processed, it also kept the consumer's home cleaner than unsliced bread. Furthermore, it perfectly fit the new electric toasters popping up in breakfast rooms across the country. A writer in 1940 commented on the speed with which Americans embraced the new bread: "I can remember when the advent of pre-sliced bread from the bakery was the cause of many a dubious headshake from housewives. This was no more than ten years ago— probably considerably less than that. Now sliced bread is assumed. The same housewife who was doubtful about it would consider the slicing process a complete waste of time."[71]

Liberated from making (or even slicing) her family's bread, technology also liberated the American mom from apple pie. In 1905, a Pittsburgh baker introduced his pie-making machine, modeled on domestic waffle irons. The machine constructed pies in two parts, first baking crusts in iron molds, then filling and topping them with meringue. Its creator, a Mr. Louis, claimed that it could turn out 40 pies per hour. One newspaper editorialist met the news with outrage. Describing the machine's functions, this writer declared: "This is all wrong. Even a loaf of bread should have some individuality, and as for machine-made pie, it should rank in the dietetic category even lower than hash."[72] Another writer found the invention cause for celebration, announcing, "Lovers of the great American dainty—pie—will rejoice to learn that a new era has set for its unlimited production."[73]

The pie machine even moved one writer to poetry, or "Pi-lines and Pick-ups":

> New England's hands are raised in awe;
>   astonishment is rife;
> They've had a shock the likes of which
>   comes seldom in this life;
> The article of diet which they eat three
>   times a day
> Has been put out of making in the good
>   old fashioned way;
> And now they're going to turn 'em out by
>   Hundreds, slick and clean

By the help and aid, they tell us, of
   a pie machine!"[74]

Factory-made pies were not an entirely new phenomenon, but even pies made in factories had been made by hand until Mr. Louis's invention. A 1900 newspaper article noted that in New York City, "the pie business . . . has been little short of the phenomenal and it is not always possible for the factories to meet the demands for the product."[75] The "biggest pie factory" in New York was able to produce 20,000 pies in one day, and there were many smaller factories and bakeries catering to the local taste for pie. It had taken some time for New Yorkers to become accustomed to factory-produced pies, and there was "a popular prejudice against the factory pie" based in "the idea that the factory pie was turned out by machinery and was not the work of human hands." The author assured readers that each factory pie was made by a real person in an atmosphere "scrupulously clean" and therefore safe. An attempt had once been made to sell machine-made pies in New York, but the pies had been rejected by consumers and the experiment not repeated.[76] Five years later, Mr. Louis of Pittsburgh wagered that Americans could overcome their squeamishness.

Commercially produced sweets—pies, cakes, cookies, and pastries—were not as popular as factory-made bread. Partly this was because factories could only turn out a limited number of kinds of sweets because it was too expensive to have machinery and space to produce a variety as wide as what the home baker could produce. Transportation for baked goods was also more difficult, as they tend to be more delicate than a simple loaf of bread. It may also be, as has been argued, that although women were happy enough to give up the hard work of making bread—a very ordinary product—they continued to take personal pride in the desserts that families perceived as treats.[77]

During World War II, processed food companies faced some of the same problems as those of appliance manufacturers. Military demand for food as well as metals limited the quantities of canned foods they could make available to the domestic market. Del Monte admitted that shoppers might find their company's products in short supply in local groceries, but emphasized their claim that whatever there *was* would be of good quality.[78] During the shortages of World War II, one food processing company, B&M, suggested that if consumers could not find their brand of baked beans in the market, they should go home and "bake your beans at home the genuine New England way" rather than settle for another brand.[79] Homemade was here presented as second to B&M but still superior to other industrially processed beans.

Some companies took advantage of the fact of shortages to subtly encourage hoarding of their products. The Van Camp company published an alarmist advertisement in January 1944 warning readers that there was likely to be a shortage of tuna in the coming year: "Recent misleading press dispatches have created the impression that there is going to be an abundance of tuna for civilian use. This is unfortunate, for it is not true."[80] War department posters of this era regularly warned citizens against the dangers of gossip, so readers would already have an idea that rumors could be dangerous. The tuna supply would be limited because all of Van Camp's "tuna clippers" were loaned to the navy, and their smaller boats were not able to compensate. This may well have been true, but the tone of the advertisement, which threatened that consumers might not always find tuna in their local markets, gave the impression that a tuna shortage was a matter of national security.

Other companies marketed their goods in relation to rationing in a more supportive tone. An ad for Gephardt's chili powder, for example, claimed: "This famous flavor helps you save points!"[81] Properly spiced, shorter supplies of meat could seem like more than they were. Likewise, Armour, a meat-processing company, offered Vitalox, a kind of sauce with "hearty beef flavor" that "makes ration-restricted dishes taste so wonderful!"[82] Finally, a thoughtful ad for Knox Gelatine asked readers "Short of Meat?" and suggested a "meat loaf" of scraps suspended in gelatin as a way to help "you stretch your proteins."[83]

NOTES

1. *Des Moines (Iowa) Homestead,* July 18, 1890, p. 7.

2. The Home Institute of the *New York Herald Tribune, America's Cook Book* (New York: Charles Scribner's Sons, 1937), p. 711.

3. Fred E. H. Schroeder, "More 'Small Things Forgotten': Domestic Electrical Plugs and Receptacles, 1881–1931," *Technology and Culture,* 27 (1986): 526.

4. Earl Lifshey, *The Housewares Story* (Chicago: National Housewares Manufacturers Association, 1973), p. 132.

5. Lifshey, *The Housewares Story,* pp. 132–33.

6. Mildred Maddocks Bentley, *Good Housekeeping's Book on the Business of Housekeeping* (New York: Good Housekeeping, 1924), p. 12.

7. Ruth Schwartz Cowan, *More Work for Mother* (New York: Basic Books, 1983), p. 132.

8. Ida Cogswell Bailey Allen, *Mrs. Allen on Cooking, Menus, Service: 2500 Recipes* (Garden City, NY: Doubleday Page, 1924), p. 603.

9. Sears, Roebuck and Company Catalog, Fall/Winter, 1935/1936, pp. 517–27.

10. Advertisement for The Gas Light and Coke Company, London, in Herman Senn, *Chafing Dish and Casserole Cookery* (London: The Food and Cookery Publishing Company, 1918), p. 86.

11. Advertisement, *Good Housekeeping*, 118 (January 1944): 93.

12. Abraham Meyerson, *The Nervous Housewife* (Boston: Little Brown and Co, 1920), p. 260.

13. Freda De Knight, *A Date with a Dish: A Cook Book of American Negro Recipes* (New York: Hermitage Press, 1948), p. 377.

14. The Home Institute of the *New York Herald Tribune, America's Cook Book* (New York: Charles Scribner's Sons, 1937), p. v.

15. *Iowa City (Iowa) Press-Citizen*, September 7, 1926, p. 5.

16. *Charleroi (Pennsylvania) Mail*, June 21, 1929, p. 14.

17. Rhea C. Scott, *Home Labor Saving Devices* (Philadelphia: J. B. Lippincott Company, 1917), p. 39.

18. Letter from Preservance Kane, *The Housewife Magazine*, 25, no. 4 (September, 1908): 25.

19. Lifshey, *The Housewares Story*, pp. 255–59.

20. Advertisement for Vaughn Electric Co., *Decatur (Illinois) Daily Review*, February 18, 1908, p. 7.

21. Advertisement, *Good Housekeeping*, 118, no. 1 (January 1944): 153.

22. Florence Brobeck, *Cook It in a Casserole* (New York: M. Barrows and Company, 1943), p. 174.

23. "Electric Mixer Mixed Dough Fast," *(Coshocton Ohio) Democratic Standard*, September 23, 1904, p. 3.

24. Advertisement for Carl N. Owens Drugstore, *Cedar Rapids (Iowa) Evening Gazette*, February 16, 1911, p. 8.

25. *(Fort Wayne, Indiana) News-Sentinel*, August 20, 1922, p. 5.

26. Advertisement for Skagg's Safeway Stores, *Woodland (California) Daily Democrat*, September 14, 1928, p. 5.

27. "Electricity and Bachelors" *Mansfield (Ohio) News*, August 22, 1907, p. 4.

28. Janet M. Hill, *Salads, Sandwiches and Chafing Dish Dainties*, p. 157.

29. *New York Times*, June 10, 1894, Wednesday Page, p. 18.

30. Hill, *Salads, Sandwiches and Chafing Dish Dainties*, p. ix.

31. Grace Duffield Goodwin, "To My Chafing Dish," in *Chafing Dish and Casserole Cookery*, ed. Herman Senn (London: The Food and Cookery Publishing Co., 1918), p. 6.

32. Ann Taylor Burbank, "To My Mistress. By a Chafing Dish," in *Chafing Dish and Casserole Cookery*, ed. Herman Senn, p. 6.

33. Herman Senn, *Chafing Dish and Casserole Cookery*, p. 7.

34. Lifshey, *The Housewares Story*, pp. 156–57.

35. Brobeck, *Cook it in a Casserole*, p. 7.

36. Brobeck, *Cook it in a Casserole*, p. 7.

37. John van Willigen and Anne van Willigen, *Food and Everyday Life on Kentucky Family Farms, 1920–1950* (Lexington: University of Kentucky Press, 2006), p. 210.

38. van Willigen and van Willigen, *Food and Everyday Life on Kentucky Family Farms, 1920–1950*, p. 210.

39. van Willigen and van Willigen, *Food and Everyday Life on Kentucky Family Farms, 1920–1950*, p. 214.

40. Marion Harris Neil, *Canning, Preserving, and Picling* (Philadelphia: David McKay Publisher, 1914), p. 11.

41. Miriam Birdseye, Field Trip report, May 22–29, 1930, New Jersey. RG 176 Box 534 Folder "Reports—Field Trip, 1930–31," National Archives and Records Administration.

42. Harris Neil, *Canning, Preserving, and Picling*, p. 11.

43. Helen Klaas Engdahl, "Home Preservation of Food," *Journal of Home Economics*, 33, no. 10 (December, 1941): 721.

44. Upton Sinclair, *The Jungle* (1906; repr., New York: Pocket Books, 2004) p. 166.

45. Katherine A. Smith, "Labels," *Journal of Home Economics*, 16 (October, 1924), p. 554.

46. Advertisement in *Good Housekeeping*, 110, (January, 1924): 56.

47. Katherine A. Smith, "Labels on Food Packages a Safe Guide to Buyer if the Text Carefully Read," *Yearbook, United States Department of Agriculture, 1930* (Washington, D.C.: Government Printing Office, 1930), p. 339.

48. Dorothy Marsh, "Visits to the Grocer," *Good Housekeeping*, 110, no. 1 (January 1940): 112.

49. "Canned Foods Week," *American Food Journal*, 8, no. 2 (February 1913): 43.

50. Hermann Vulte, *The Food Industries* (Easton, PA: The Chemical Publishing Co., 1920), p. 201.

51. Vulte, *The Food Industries*, p. 207.

52. Vulte, *The Food Industries*, p. 208.

53. Vulte, *The Food Industries*, p. 259.

54. Advertisement, *Good Housekeeping*, 110, no. 1 (January 1940): 68.

55. David Horowitz, *Putting Meat on the American Table* (Baltimore: Johns Hopkins Press, 2006), p. 83.

56. Vulte, *The Food Industries*, pp. 247–48.

57. Horowitz, *Putting Meat on the American Table*, p. 58.

58. Horowtiz, *Putting Meat on the American Table*, p. 60.

59. Hazel Kyrk, *A Theory of Consumption* (Boston: Houghton, Mifflin Co., 1923), p. 113.

60. Advertisement, *American Food Journal*, 10, no. 1 (January, 1915): 25.

61. Public Law Number 59–384 34 Stat. 768 (1906). http://www.fda.gov/opacom/laws/wileyact.htm.

62. Helen Klaas Engdahl, "Home Preservation of Food," *Journal of Home Economics,* 33, no. 10 (December, 1941): 721.

63. Advertisement, *American Food Journal,* 1, no. 10 (October, 1906): 32.

64. Nancy Tomes, *The Gospel of Germs* (Cambridge, MA: Harvard University Press, 1998), p. 169.

65. William G. Panschar, *Baking in America,* Vol. I, *Economic Development* (Evanston, IL: Northwestern University Press, 1956), p. 82.

66. "Meddling with Legitimate Business," *American Food Journal,* 10, no. 3 (March 1915): 93.

67. Panschar, *Baking in America,* p. 69.

68. Panschar, *Baking in America,* pp. 93–94.

69. Panschar, *Baking in America,* p. 99.

70. Advertisement for Home Bakery, *Spirit Lake (Iowa) Beacon,* May 4, 1933, p. 4.

71. *Mason City (Iowa) Globe-Gazette,* January 5, 1940, p. 4.

72. *The Evening World* (New York), August 12, 1905 evening ed., p. 6.

73. "Better Pies Than Mother's Turned Out by Machinery," *Oakland (California) Tribune,* July 10, 1905, p. 7.

74. "Pi-lines and Pick-ups," *Los Angeles* (California) *Herald,* September 2, 1905, p. 4.

75. "Growth of the Pie Habit," *Nebraska State Journal,* June 25, 1900, p. 3.

76. "Growth of the Pie Habit," *Nebraska State Journal,* June 25, 1900, p. 3.

77. William G. Paschar, *Baking in America,* p. 100.

78. Advertisement in *Good Housekeeping,* 118, no. 1 (January 1944): 77.

79. Advertisement in *Good Housekeeping,* 118, no. 1 (January 1944): 160.

80. Advertisement in *Good Housekeeping,* 118, no. 1 (January 1944): 96.

81. Advertisement in *Good Housekeeping,* 118, no. 1 (January 1944): 159.

82. Advertisement in *Good Housekeeping,* 118, no. 2 (February 1944): 78.

83. Advertisement in *Good Housekeeping,* 118, no. 1 (January 1944): 112.

CHAPTER 4
EATING HABITS

In her memoir of a life of dieting, novelist Fannie Hurst hungrily recalled the breakfasts of her youth. Born in Ohio, in 1899, Hurst remembered, "Oatmeal in a covered dish was served out with plentiful additions of butter, sugar and yellowish cream. A platter of bacon and eggs . . . toast or hot biscuits or both arrived in a wicker basket, all tucked in under a red-and-white napkin with a fringed edge. There was usually hominy or grits or stacks of griddle cakes with apple jelly or molasses. Coffee and plenty of it . . . and, more often than not, crumb coffee cake, still hot, and thickly sprinkled with cinnamon and sugar."[1] In 1935, however, such a breakfast was hard to come by, especially in urban areas. It had become fashionable to breakfast on just a cup of coffee and a roll. Hurst suggested that this was a northeastern custom that had spread to the Midwest. Attempting to lose weight, Hurst had had to abandon the beloved morning repast: "I was reared to like breakfast. I still like breakfast. Heaven my witness, I have not eaten a breakfast in twelve years."

BREAKFAST

Hurst was not alone in recognizing the transformation of breakfast, nor in eating less. The shift from a large meal not substantively different from any other meal of the day, to a smaller meal associated especially with eggs and cereals, was already underway in 1898 when a writer for the *Delineator Magazine* noted: "Meat for breakfast is not as often provided for the matutinal meal as formerly," matutinal

referring to the morning. This author advocated taking a light breakfast in the summer, "a bit of fruit, a cup of coffee, a slice of toast and
a small dish of some cereal being quite sufficient for any appetite."[2] A
small breakfast became associated with the new culture of profession-
alism and the science of management. The entrepreneur of the 20th
century had no time to waste on lavish morning meals. A journalist
referred to "the businessman who makes his breakfast of coffee and a
sweet roll," as a commonly recognized figure in American life. Where
the rhythms of life were a little slower, however, the custom of a larger
breakfast apparently lingered. The author of a cookbook about the
cuisine of the social elites of coastal Georgia prefaced her recipe for
"a good hash" by stating: "In the South, where some people are still
guilty of eating a comfortable breakfast, this economical receipt is
very popular."[3]

Dressed somewhat inappropriately for the occasion, President
Theodore Roosevelt breakfasted in 1903 with a group of cowboys,
serving himself from pots placed close to the fire, in Hugo,
Colorado. According to Roosevelt, his days on a ranch gave him
a taste for such cuisine, which featured stewed beans and beef.
(Courtesy of Library of Congress.)

A breakfast menu from the Hotel Manhattan in New York offered diners in 1900 a range of options, from the 35-cent breakfast of coffee or tea and a roll and butter to the deluxe $1 breakfast of coffee, rolls, chicken hash or a small steak with bacon and potatoes and hominy with cream. Nineteen years later, at the Venice Cafeteria, near the beach in Venice, California, the hungry could assemble their own breakfast from a wide variety of fresh fruits, cereals, pancakes, bacon, ham, and sausage.[4] In the 1920s, the Brae Mar Inn, in Santa Monica, offered six "Special Club Breakfasts," which presumably brought together popular combinations. For 20 cents, a diner could enjoy "hot cakes and coffee," or for 15 cents more "hamburger, one egg, potatoes, toast, and coffee."[5] For those who lived outside the borders of polite society, breakfast might consist, as it did for Theodore Roosevelt on his ranch, of "a cup of coffee and some mouthfuls of bread and jerked elk meat."[6]

The popularization of breakfast cereals, begun in the late 19th century, facilitated the shrinking of breakfast. Quaker Oats's campaign to convince American consumers that its product was "the ideal breakfast" dish succeeded quite well. Cold breakfast cereals became even more popular as advances in packaging reassured consumers that the product was sanitary. Cereal eating also fit well with the recommendations of public health experts who encouraged Americans to use more milk and whole grains. First introduced by food faddists in the mid-19th century, the boxed cereal served with cold milk became an all-American staple food by the mid-20th century. Although breakfast required less and less work to produce, it remained the one meal that most Americans routinely ate at home. Although it became more common to eat lunch and dinner out, the morning meal of oatmeal or a plate of eggs and toast stayed private at least through the end of World War II.

For some Americans, smaller meals were not the result of changing trends but of economic hardship. A widowed mother of four who had turned to the Federated Charities of Baltimore for help wrote up, at their request, a week's worth of her family menus. To the horror of her social workers, the list revealed a Monday breakfast of bread and butter, a Tuesday breakfast of "ballony" and a Wednesday breakfast of "downuts."[7]

Culture and circumstances both shaped what was available for breakfast. As a visitor to the remote Wyoming home of a Mexican American couple, Elinore Pruitt Stewart was offered a breakfast of tortillas, cheese, and butter with hot coffee mellowed with goat's milk. Although she was happy to have this meal, Stewart's own ideal

In 1918, when this youngster enjoyed a breakfast of Quaker Puffed Rice, prepared breakfast cereals were still something of a novelty. (Courtesy of Library of Congress.)

breakfast was "pork and beans heated in a frying-pan on a camp fire." To enjoy this meal properly, "You must be away out in Wyoming, with the morning sun just gilding the distant peaks and your pork and beans must be out of a can, heated in a disreputable old frying pan, served with coffee *boiled* in a battered old pail and drunk from a tomato-can." Once a person had tasted these delicacies, "You'll *never* want iced melons, powdered sugar, and fruit or sixty-nine varieties of breakfast food," the staples of fashionable urban breakfast tables again.[8]

LUNCH

As breakfasts became smaller and speedier, the character of lunch also changed significantly. The urbanization of American life and establishment of a national public school system meant that fewer families ate lunch together. Children ate at school while fathers, typically still primary breadwinners for their families, took short breaks to eat lunch near their work places. Working class men and women bought their lunches from lunch carts that parked outside of factories or brought their own meals in metal lunch boxes or paper bags. Generally these lunches consisted of leftovers, sometimes packaged as sandwiches.

Those who worked in offices took their lunch in newly ubiquitous lunch restaurants. In 1916, a guide for visitors of New York City explained, "A great majority of restaurants in the downtown business and financial sections are exclusively for men, are open during business hours only, and a considerable portion of them are of the 'quick lunch' order," meaning that owners spent little money creating a pleasant ambience and patrons spent little time thinking about it.[9] Where businessmen of previous generations might have lunched at saloons or in private clubs, the heavy food and alcohol associated with such venues began to seem antithetical to the new business style of speed and efficiency.

Lunch counters opened to serve the busy office worker. In 1891, entrepreneur Charles Palmer patented a food wagon known as the "owl." The owls, which appeared at night on the streets of Worcester,

Construction workers take a lunch break on a steel beam atop the RCA Building at Rockefeller Center, New York, 1932. In the foreground, a worker reaches into his metal lunchbox. (AP Photo.)

Massachusetts, to serve night workers, "featured a small counter with stools" for customers.[10] Other businessmen quickly picked up on Palmer's idea and set up more permanent lunch counters throughout the cities of the Northeast. Some, hoping to suggest a higher quality of meal, used railroad dining cars, traditionally called diners, as restaurants, setting them up in lots that provided for parking in the back. The look of the detached dining car was so appealing that it became a popular style even for establishments that had never seen the rails.[11] Inside the diners the grill took up one side of the building, allowing customers to see their eggs and bacon or burgers frying and so to be assured that their food would come quickly and that there were no unappetizing secrets behind the kitchen door.

In Philadelphia in 1902, the partnership of Horn and Hardart opened a new kind of restaurant, based on an idea first pioneered in Germany, which they called the automat. Applying the mania for efficiency to food service, and addressing fears of contaminated foods, the

In the 1910s, men at work in nearby factories and offices in downtown Manhattan bought lunch from hot dog stands such as pictured. A sign on the building behind the stands advertises a lunchroom where food could be bought in a slightly more genteel atmosphere. (Courtesy of Library of Congress.)

automat appeared to dispense hygienic, ready-made meals magically as if from a machine. Customers paid first, buying nickels that they then slipped into slots next to small glass compartments that displayed cold food items. Once the nickel dropped, a door opened, and the food could be removed. Hot food was dispensed from steam tables. Among the more than 400 menu items served at various branches of the automat were foods thought of as "American," including sandwiches, pies, soups, macaroni and cheese, and a version of traditional New England baked beans that earned special popularity. The novelty of the automat drew large crowds and the speed of service and relatively low prices, to which no tip needed to be added, attracted a loyal following among those who worked nearby.

At the same time that cities developed business districts, in the last quarter of the 19th century, shopping neighborhoods also emerged. Middle class women began to leave their suburban and residential neighborhoods during the daytime to shop in the new department stores, designed with their preferences in mind. Some of the new stores, like Wanamaker's, which had stores in both Philadelphia and New York, opened lunchrooms. Placing the restaurant inside the store

Postcard of an automat dining room at 1557 Broadway, Manhattan. (AP Photo/HO/Courtesy of The Museum of the City of New York.)

enabled the business to keep its customers present and to fortify them for more shopping. Stores with no restaurants risked losing the hungry consumer as she went elsewhere to eat.

A 1906 menu from a Wanamaker's Tea Room lists fare that was considered ladylike such as lobster salad, chicken croquettes, shirred eggs, an assortment of pastries including éclairs and macaroons, and 10 kinds of ice cream. There was not a steak, chop, or potato to be found on the list.[12] The Siegel Cooper shopper who felt the need of refreshment while browsing in this New York City store could fortify herself with a wide variety of sandwiches, including the hearty hot roast beef sandwich with potato salad and the more dainty lettuce sandwich. She also had the choice of 31 pastries and desserts, 10 kinds of pie, 9 flavors of ice cream, and 8 varieties of "fragrant teas."[13] R. H. Macy and Co., soon to be known simply as Macy's, offered a simple afternoon tea of "assorted sandwiches," marmalade, macaroons, lady fingers, Uneeda biscuits, and ice cream.[14] At the fashionable penthouse tearoom at Bullock's department store in Los Angeles, a menu from 1938 shows the influence of fad diets. Diners could choose from pear halves with cottage cheese, avocado, and rye krisp or a "vitamin salad" of raw carrot, raisin, and apples. Both the "Westwood Chicken Salad" and the tuna salad sandwich were served with pineapple, reflecting the growing fondness for pineapple on the American mainland and its high standing among diet experts.[15]

Independent tearooms also opened in shopping districts to serve the "refined" lady shopper. A 1916 visitor's guide to New York City noted: "During the past few years tea rooms have sprung up all over the city, usually low in price with service a la carte." Meals in these establishments were "almost invariably good, but the portions are likely to be small," as cultural norms dictated that respectable women were not to be seen eating hearty meals in public.[16] Supporting the notion that tearooms were places for women to eat light meals, the guidebook noted that New York's "fashionable tea rooms are open throughout the afternoon, but are most frequented between 4:30 and 5."[17] Mandel's Tea Room in Chicago hosted gatherings of women's clubs as well as serving drop-in customers. Middle class women, careful of their reputations, might initially have been reluctant to be seen eating in public, so tearooms served as a welcome oasis of gentility in the bustle of city spaces. The meals they served were light and included many sweets, suggesting that the women who dined in these establishments were in the market only for treats, not true sustenance. In part this protected them from appearing to have animal natures, and in part it suggested that they had servants at home to prepare

Patrons in this typical diner, the White Tower in Amsterdam, New York, could buy a bowl of soup for 15 cents, a piece of pie for 10 cents, or a hamburger for 5 cents. People of all ages felt comfortable in such establishments. (Courtesy of Library of Congress.)

their real meals. Any woman who did not have a servant clearly also did not have time to spend the afternoon shopping and snacking.

Tearooms also served the first generation of female office workers, young women who had a social status slightly higher than that of factory workers but still far below that of the leisured shopping class. Tearooms gave these young women a space in which to enjoy a midday meal without exposing themselves to the eyes of possibly lecherous businessmen and male clerks. Those who did not mind mixed-gender meals also frequented city lunchrooms like Edward F. Lang's Ladies' and Gents' Lunchroom in New York. There men and women could both choose from an eclectic menu rich in fish, shellfish, and "roasts, etc., etc," which included an entire New England boiled dinner as well as chops, roast turkey, and corned beef hash. Diners could also have eggs prepared many ways, five styles of fried potatoes, and a huge assortment of puddings, pies, cakes, and ice creams, including "lunch cake," a dense raisin cake flavored with nutmeg, cinnamon, and cloves. Despite the establishment's claim to serve "Ladies and Gents," Lang's menu included the statement "Guests are requested to keep an eye"— with the eye represented graphically—"on their Garments" lest someone of lesser dignity made off with an unwatched coat or handbag.[18]

By the early 1920s, tearooms and lunchrooms had both become interesting new business opportunities for women trained in institutional management, a subfield of home economics. Two articles on the topic of opening such establishments were published in one 1923 issue of the *Journal of Home Economics*, and the two co-deans of the home economics department at Cornell University actually opened their own tea room, perhaps to serve as models to their students.

On the days when they did not visit the city to browse through department stores, middle class ladies often lunched together in their own homes. Sometimes they issued formal invitations and made the meal part of an afternoon spent playing cards. Other occasions were more casual. Because husbands no longer returned home for the midday meal, women had the opportunity of serving foods not considered "masculine," and distinct food habits emerged around these female meals. A cookbook published in 1903 by a group of women in Cleveland, Ohio, suggested a "Menu for a few friends" composed of "Peanut wafers, cream sponge cake, chocolate with whipped cream, pineapple lemonade."[19]

Because their culture operated under a common assumption that men demanded meat at every meal and that men disliked decorative elements in food, American women's lunches seem to have gone in the opposite direction, celebrating sweetness and fluff. Many included elaborately composed gelatin salads topped with dollops of mayonnaise mixed with whipped cream. Preparing these meals for others who they knew would appreciate them perhaps served as a creative outlet for some women. Middle class women's lunch choices may also have been affected by the fact that until the 1920s, most wore corsets that tightly confined their stomachs, making the pork chop lunch seem somewhat less appealing than the dish of whipped cream. Both might be equally fattening, but the whipped cream could be consumed more comfortably.

A cookbook titled *Dining for Moderns*, published in 1940, proclaimed: "The times of large, formal luncheons have long passed. The smartest women in town serve the simplest and lightest luncheons." These "smart women" the author suggested, might enjoy "eggs Orientale," a dish of deviled eggs stuffed with anchovies, lemon, olives, and nuts covered in a white sauce flavored with Worcestershire sauce, mushrooms, and shrimp. This light luncheon dish was best accompanied by a green salad and finished with a piece of chocolate cake.[20] Etiquette expert Emily Post agreed that simplicity had come to be the preferred style in American foodways. In 1937, she wrote: "We of this modern day are inclined to find our ideal of hospitality in simple rather than in formal party giving." This shift to simplicity, however, should not mean lowered standards of gentility. "The ideal menu," she argued, "whether it be that of a formal dinner or the little dinner for six or eight—should be notable not for the number of its courses but for the excellence of a few dishes which are well balanced as well as satisfying." Modernism's reverence for utility had seemingly influenced American food habits, at least for the upper middle class, who were Post's presumed audience.[21]

For the "Bridge Luncheon," a popular social event for middle class women during the first half of the 20th century, one cookbook author suggested the following menu: "Cream of mushroom soup (in petites marmites); melba toast; frozen tomato salad; Roquefort cheese biscuits; ambrosia; coffee."[22] The lunch would be followed by an afternoon playing bridge in foursomes, a way for women living somewhat isolated lives to find both companionship and competitive entertainment. Yet despite the many elaborate menus for lunches published in magazines and cookbooks, Christine Terhune Herrick revealed that it was a "'picked-up' luncheon that obtains in so many homes." Herrick advocated against this habit "which consists of a bite hastily snatched in pantry or kitchen by each member of the family, as it suits his or her convenience." Perhaps because formal meals seemed to require the kinds of guide books by which she made her living, Herrick implored her readers to sit down to a "dainty" table for lunch whether there was to be company or not.[23]

From the beginning of the 20th century forward, increasing numbers of American schoolchildren could expect to receive lunch at school. For some, from poor families, lunch was free; for others it was purchased for a small fee. In 1925, schoolchildren in New York City could expect to choose from the following: a soup, usually milk based; one or two hot dishes such as spaghetti with tomato sauce or scalloped potatoes, baked beans, or a hot roast beef sandwich. Meat was "not served except in made up dishes where it flavors potatoes or rice." Students were also offered potato, egg, green vegetable, or fruit salad, and could choose one of five sandwiches. Fillings included meat, cheese, jam, peanut butter, and lettuce with mayonnaise. Reinforcing gender stereotypes, one writer remarked, "Boys like heavy meat sandwiches thickly cut," while girls "prefer jam, lettuce, and cream cheese sandwiches thinly cut and daintily served." Both boys and girls could

Through the end of World War II, it was common for adults to drink coffee with every meal. Here a woman sets the table with all of the foods that will be eaten. According to the photographer, this meal in New Mexico included "home-cured ham and gravy, pinto beans, corn, homemade pickles, homegrown tomatoes, homemade bread and hot biscuits, fruit salad, cake," and two kinds of pie. (Russell Lee, Courtesy of Library of Congress.)

finish their meals with a baked pudding, ice cream, plain cake, or fresh fruit every day.[24]

It was not until the School Lunch Act of 1946 that state lunch programs were required to work with trained dietitians to ensure that school lunches were nutritionally balanced. Until then, lunch menus were largely the choice of school cooks who typically worked to keep costs low and preparation simple. For millions of mothers, school lunch programs made life easier and for millions of children they provided a steady source of nutrition, especially important during the lean years of the Great Depression.

DINNER

Just as breakfasts became smaller over the first half of the 20th century, dinners, too, appear to have shrunk. Emily Post thought that it might have been a result of voluntary rationing during World War I, "which accustomed every one to going with very little meat and to marked reduction in all food," or it might be due to the new reduction diet fads that were "causing even grandparents to aspire to svelte figures." Whatever the cause, it seemed clear to her that "People are putting much less food on their tables than formerly." Even the "very rich, living in the biggest houses with the largest array of servants" seldom went beyond four courses by 1922.[25]

In contrast, in 1899, the Bingham House Hotel in Philadelphia offered a New Year's Day dinner that greeted the last year of the 19th century with a feast of rich foods and multiple courses. After an appetizer of blue point oysters, guests at the hotel were offered a game soup, salmon "genoise" (served in a rich brown sauce), lobster gratinee, sweetbreads baked in puff pastry, prime rib, turkey, and cauliflower in hollandaise sauce. The meal then paused for "New Year's Punch," only to continue with quail and blackberry jam and a selection of desserts that included plum pudding with cognac sauce, cherry pie, champagne jelly, and "fancy cake."[26] This kind of feasting would go out of fashion over the next 20 years, as would the fascination with dishes that were identified with foreign countries, especially France. American dinners, even on special occasions, would become more modest and more local in inspiration.

When the Boston Red Sox won the World Series in 1912, owner George Putnam threw a celebratory dinner that took this local-food trend to a humorous extreme. Each dish was named after a player. The meal included Blue Points Stahl Style (manager), Nunamaker celery (outfielder), Fresh Putnam Farm Chicken a la Wagner (shortstop), Bradley Jelly (first base), Sweet Potatoes Bedient Style (starting pitcher), Frozen Pudding Cady Style (catcher), and Pape Coffee (relief pitcher).[27]

Mary Lockwood Matthews, a professor of home economics, offered dinner planning guidance for the more modest daily meals of middle class homemakers in her book *Foods and Cookery*. Matthews explained that dinner "in most homes is the 'heaviest' meal served during the day because it usually consists of a greater variety of food than the other two."[28] Because the majority of married women did not work outside the home in this period, there was perhaps the expectation that dinner could be more elaborate than other meals because a housewife had all day to prepare it. Matthews informed readers that it was not necessary to serve soup at the beginning of every dinner, nor dessert at its end.[29] That she felt the need to mention this suggests that most of her readers would have assumed the opposite—that a proper dinner began with soup and ended with a sweet. She was also quite adamant that "only one kind of *meat* should be served" at dinner, rejecting American traditions in which an evening meal might be made up of several kinds of meat, such as a roast chicken and a ham with perhaps also a fish dish.[30] She also warned against too many different vegetables, suggesting that two were sufficient. Most important, "No person should spend too large a share of her time in cooking, as there are other things as important to be done."[31] The idea that there was anything as important or even more important for a woman to do than cook for her family was still quite new in this era when women had only just won the right to vote.

Working class homemakers, while struggling to make do with less, seem to have shared wealthier women's understanding of what dishes constituted a proper dinner. A study of the food habits of the families of steel workers in Pennsylvania revealed sample dinner menus. On Monday one family ate "meat, beans, potatoes, fruit, red beets, pickle," and on Wednesday enjoyed "lamb stew with dumplings, cucumber, eggplant, beans, corn, coffee, bread and butter, fruit."[32]

While advocating for decorousness and dignity at the family dinner table, domestic expert Christine Terhune Herrick offered a portrait of what she considered the all-too-common reality of these meals: "At the end of a dinner, how many family tables look neat and orderly? Do they not rather appear to have been shaken up by an earthquake shock? At each place the soiled dishes are pushed to one side or stacked in forbidding disorder." Among the detritus of the table, Herrick listed a meat platter (shockingly not cleared before the dessert was served), more than one vegetable dish, "catsup bottles, cruets, carafes and similar articles," crusts of bread and an assortment of dirty forks, knives, and spoons. From Herrick's portrait, it can be gleaned that typical middle class family meals included several vegetables, meat, bread, and assorted condiments. The cruet, a holder typically used to bring salad dressings to a table, suggests the presence of some kind of fresh greens or other raw fruits or vegetables.[33]

In many communities, the largest meal of the week was the Sunday dinner, to which guests were sometimes invited. Served slightly earlier in the day than the typical dinner, Sunday dinner and its bounty reflected the fact that many Christian Americans observed the Sabbath by staying home but not by ceasing all work. For mill workers in Homestead, Pennsylvania, "Sunday dinner is the one meal that serves as a time of festivity." A researcher found that in "almost every" home "on Sunday an extra piece of meat, usually a roast, was bought. The men have more leisure on Sunday and sit down with pleasure to a more elaborate meal."[34] Similarly, a study of working class families in Buffalo noted that families of Polish ancestry typically served a whole chicken for Sunday dinner, marking that meal as special.[35]

The characters in a young adult novel about life in a small town in Minnesota at the beginning of the 20th century typically enjoyed a Sunday dinner of "duck with apple dressing, dumplings, brown gravy, served with butter drenched sweet potatoes and often topped off with an apple pie which came to the table under a crown of whipped cream."[36] As was the case in many small towns and rural areas, the duck enjoyed at this meal had been shot by the father of the family.

In 1912, one writer suggested that the Sunday dinner was often used to showcase the talents of a family's young women for prospective suitors. "After a young man who has been eating his lunches at a dairy lunch," the author began, referring to some of the chain lunch restaurants that had recently appeared in urban areas, "is invited to take Sunday dinner with the family once or twice, and is casually told that 'Katherine made these biscuits' or 'Katherine baked this cake,' he is in a frame of mind to become a 'prospect'" for Katherine's choice in marriage.[37] As the introduction of the automobile and cinema allowed young people to perform their courtships outside the family home, such scenes became less frequent, but the Sunday dinner maintained its status as the most important family meal during the week.

MEALS IN TRANSIT

The 20th-century introduction of two new forms of transportation—the car and the airplane—affected American eating habits, creating new expectations and new opportunities. When the first Ford Model A automobiles hit the roads, the roads were hardly ready for them. Lack of uniform surfacing was a big problem for enthusiastic early adopters of motoring and so was lunch. By the end of the 19th century, Americans had become accustomed to making long journeys by rail. Trains usually included dining cars, but many passengers brought their own picnics anyway to save money. Either way, Americans had grown accustomed to eating while in motion.

Where roadside inns had once flourished in the days of coach travel, their numbers had dwindled significantly by the time automobile travel began. Thus early motorists had to carry their own food, sometimes with comic-tragic results as portrayed in *The Motor Girls on a Tour,* one in a popular series of books about a young women's auto club. As one member of the club took a turn too sharply, her picnic hamper fell out and was then run over by another of the club's members. "Bent and crippled enameled dishes from the lately fine and completely equipped auto-hamper were scattered about in all directions. Here and there a piece of pie could be identified, while the chicken sandwiches were mostly recognizable by the fact that a newly arrived yellow dog persistently gnawed at one or two particular mud spots."[38]

For those who dared not risk their picnic baskets to wild driving, roadside restaurants began to appear. Because "early automobile travel remained the privilege of the well-to-do," however, "the earliest roadside eateries catered especially to the gentry." This meant that they took the form of tearooms where only tea and sweets, rather than hearty meals and alcohol, were served in a genteel atmosphere. Many of these tearooms were set up in the parlors of picturesque farmhouses in landscapes that served as destinations for the motorist.[39]

As advances in production technology made it possible to sell more cars at lower prices, the car became a convenience and pleasure for

When automobiles became affordable for ordinary Americans, they became part of social life. This group on a company outing in Washington, D.C. has driven right up to their picnic spot. (Courtesy of Library of Congress.)

By 1939, Americans had grown accustomed to being able to grab a quick bite to eat at places like the hamburger stand pictured here in Texas. (Courtesy of Library of Congress.)

Americans of the middle and lower middle class, as well as the elite. Salesmen driving from town to town on business or families making long trips to visit relatives required food in less remote and less fussy settings than the tearooms offered. For this market, roadside stands, usually just simple shacks with large service windows, began to pop up along the highway. To capture attention, many of these were built in unusual shapes such as windmills, oranges, hot dogs, or milk bottles.[40] Roadside shacks served simple, quickly prepared foods like ice cream and hamburgers. Because the shack itself provided no seating, diners ate in their cars, in some cases from trays brought out to them by "car hops."

The more commonplace cars became, the more amenities arose to serve drivers. Gas stations and motels began to appear along roadsides, and many of them included small restaurants to help travelers refuel their stomachs for long journeys. These sit-down restaurants served simple food but offered three distinct meals, rather than one menu of snacks all day. In addition, most offered baked goods such as cakes and pies that could make something slightly special out of an otherwise ordinary meal. The distinctive chrome-plated diners that had become commonplace in city streets and around factory neighborhoods by the 1920s also moved out to the edges of highways to provide drivers with the same kind of predictably simple, cheap, fast food they were coming to expect to find in transit.

The roadside market offered special opportunities for chain food businesses. Traveling long distances from home, Americans who might feel nervous about the local fare would be thrilled to see a familiar sign alerting them to a standardized food experience. If one had eaten at Howard Johnson's in one's hometown, for example, one could safely bet that there would be the same things to eat in a Howard Johnson's 500 miles from home. No need to risk one's stomach on the local cuisine. Howard Johnson was one of the first entrepreneurs to franchise roadside "family restaurants." His orange-roofed buildings gave travelers a bright visual clue that they were close to food they would recognize. As more people traveled by car and more stopped at chains like Howard Johnson's, "specialties" of these regional or national businesses became fixed in popular consciousness so that a driver approaching one of the orange roofs in the Midwest might find his or her mouth watering for Howard Johnson's famous fried clams, no matter that he or she was hundreds of miles from the ocean.

In the early 1930s, some chain restaurants offered customers a new style of dining—"all you can eat." For a modest 65 cents to a $1, the American diner could live out "the small boy's dream come true" and order as much of whatever he liked as his stomach could hold. By 1932, as the Great Depression deepened, this scheme had brought more than 1 million extra customers per month to one chain that instituted it. Because restaurant owners assumed, correctly, that most people would not actually take a second helping of their main dish, it offered a "pulmotor" or driving mechanism, "designed to keep the restaurant business alive through the present crisis." One restaurant manager claimed that customers occasionally participated in "an eating race," with friends. At one such event, the winner consumed "three tomato juice cocktails, three plates of chicken soup, two orders of roast beef, two orders of French fried potatoes, two orders of vegetables, an order of halibut, an order of roast veal, a vegetable dinner, three portions of lettuce and tomato salad, two portions of apple pie a la mode, a piece of chocolate layer cake, two glasses of milk and two cups of coffee." This hearty eater wanted to continue with a piece of coconut cake but was advised, for his health, to stop.[41]

The new dining style also allowed the astute observer to learn what Americans really liked to eat, within the range of choices offered. Eating contests aside, portions were not significantly larger. One researcher noted: "Among the meats, for instance, about the same proportions of

beef, lamb, and veal are taken as before." The only noticeable difference for most people was that they ate more desserts, particularly en-
joying treats such as gingerbread and steamed puddings that seemed
"old fashioned." This author attributed the craving for desserts "like
mother used to make" to the anxiety of the times.[42] Afraid of the future, diners feasted on nostalgia with whipped cream on top.

AIRPLANE FOOD

When commercial airplane travel began in the 1920s, passengers
were lucky to receive a cold sandwich from the crew for sustenance.
Airlines, however, quickly realized that they could make their service
more competitive with other means of travel by providing hot meals.
As a writer for the *New York Times* noted in 1936: "One of the criti-
cisms which airline operators have taken most to heart has been that
directed against the lack of creature comforts on airplanes," for those
"who can afford" the high prices "charged by air transport are usually
rather particular about their travel accommodations." To serve this
desirable clientele, American airlines were now attempting to catch up
with the British airlines that had already dedicated much attention to
luxury. The article described a new airplane under production by the
Douglas aircraft company. It would have "a galley for cooking and a
buffet-bar for the lines that wish to serve drinks."[43] Despite the descrip-
tion, however, the galley "kitchens" of most airplanes were not places
where food was prepared but simply places to keep it warm. In 1945,
Maxson Food Systems developed a complete frozen meal that could be
reheated in flight, but until then, food was loaded onto the planes hot
enough to eat and kept at this temperature until it was served.

As one article on meals in transit explained, "At certain stops the
planes take on meals in boxes, one for each passenger, to be issued on
trays by the stewardess. Coffee, tea, hot drinks, and soups are kept
in vacuum containers." To provide these meals, "the airlines make
contracts with restaurateurs or caterers." Although most other meals
are eaten in leisurely fashion among the clouds," an exception was
made in Kansas City where "there is a twenty minute grounding for
breakfast."[44] The article noted that bus companies had begun to try to
compete with this luxurious method of travel by providing free meals
to riders at stops along the route.

As this article suggests, airlines first bought their food from restaurants, hotels, and caterers near the airport. By the late 1930s, however,
many had opened "flight kitchens" at airports where trained food

service professionals designed and cooked meals that could travel well in thermoses and insulated boxes. Stews and meat pies were common options for hot food. Salads of many kinds were also popular with food service providers, as they did not need to be heated before being served. In 1937, the *Journal of Home Economics* announced that United Airlines had appointed what *Business Week* termed a "Maitre d'Airline" to manage the company's "four food bases on the coast-to-coast route and buying and menu planning are to be centralized to ensure variety."[45]

The director of food service for United Airlines explained some of the unique problems of in-flight dining to a New York audience in 1939. A reporter who attended the talk learned that: "At 5,000 feet in the air it takes six minutes to boil a three-minute egg. Hot coffee packed in a thermos bottle for an airplane lunch is wont to expand rapidly and blow off the cork. Milk had better be drunk quickly because it curdles almost instantaneously. Freshly baked rolls will be dry as a bone within a matter of minutes and dire things happen to inferior fruits and vegetables in the high altitudes of airplane travel."[46] By 1939, however, many of the problems had been resolved and à la carte orders could be filled, provided, of course, that they were placed long in advance when the ticket was purchased and not spontaneously thousands of miles above any functional stove.

NATIONAL HOLIDAYS

Thanksgiving

Americans first began celebrating Thanksgiving as a national holiday in the aftermath of the Civil War. It had been proposed as a way to heal the rift between regions, establishing a common tradition. All presidents after Lincoln called annually for a day of Thanksgiving to be observed on the last Thursday in November. It was not until the Great Depression that the date was shifted to the fourth Thursday in the month as an attempt by President Franklin D. Roosevelt to extend the Christmas holiday shopping season and help the struggling consumer goods industries. Through the last quarter of the 19th century, the menu slowly became established as one that featured prominently foods native to North America. Thus turkey, cranberry sauce, cornbread stuffing, sweet potatoes, and pumpkin pie graced most Thanksgiving menus by the end of the century. Many other dishes, however, were also found on these tables. Menus reveal that foods

President Franklin D. Roosevelt starts to carve the turkey in a Thanksgiving celebration, 1941. Roosevelt signed a bill establishing Thanksgiving as a national holiday to be celebrated on the fourth Thursday in November. (AP Photo.)

traditionally associated with feasts, such as beef roasts, mince pies, and plum puddings continued to tempt those who enjoyed their Thanksgiving feasts in restaurants across the country at the turn of the century. When the members of the Beta Theta Pi fraternity at Dickinson College in Pennsylvania celebrated Thanksgiving in 1892, they did so with a feast of chicken soup, creamed salmon, turkey, rice fritters, celery, Saratoga potatoes (deep fried sliced potatoes), cranberry sauce, frappe, chicken croquettes, peas, lobster salad, pumpkin custard, ice cream, cake, and coffee, apparently in that bewildering order.[47]

Americans aboard the Japanese steamship Hong Kong Maru, on their way to Honolulu or the Philippines, could celebrate their national feast day in 1900 with terrapin soup, a leg of mutton in caper sauce, a saddle of lamb with jelly, and tutti frutti ice cream or go the newly traditional route with turkey and cranberry sauce, baked sweet potatoes, and a piece of apple pie.[48] By the time America entered World

War II, however, the menu for this annual celebration had, like menus for more ordinary dinners, shrunk. In 1931, the federal Bureau of Home Economics sent out a bulletin encouraging families to replace the expensive turkey with chicken or rabbit. Food experts Hazel Stiebeling and Florence King had studied the problem and found that "while turkey might go farther in providing several meals, the cash outlay was more than many families desired to spend." Thus, as one reporter commented, "Turkeys thankful this year as chickens rule the platter." With the celebratory chicken or rabbit, Stiebeling and King suggested serving mashed potatoes, diced turnips, cranberry sauce, celery, and pumpkin pie.[49]

Once America entered World War II in 1941, many women took jobs outside the home to support the war effort. Cooking the expected feast may have seemed more daunting than in previous years. The cookbook *Double-Quick Cooking* noted: "Every woman at the head of a household has a sense of pride that almost compels her to serve a traditional Thanksgiving and Christmas dinner. Difficult as this may be for a part-time homemaker, it can be done with minimum effort and in half the time." The shortcuts included speeding up the turkey's cooking time by cutting the bird in half, and cooking the stuffing separately.[50] A 1943 painting by Norman Rockwell that portrayed the archetypal Thanksgiving dinner features little aside from a large turkey. Raw celery sticks, a few pickles, fresh fruit, and a bowl of jelly are visible, as is one covered dish, presumably holding a vegetable, but the table does not seem to groan with the kind of bounty found on tables in an earlier era.

Caterer Paul Pierce declared: "Thanksgiving is the pie season *par excellence*" and suggested throwing a pie party to make proper "use of this American product."[51] Thanksgiving pies reflected regional variations as late as 1960, when well-known food writer Clementine Paddleford wrote, "Tell me where your grandmother came from and I can tell you how many kinds of pie you serve for Thanksgiving." New Englanders enjoyed pumpkin, mince, and cranberry, occasionally including a fourth—the Marlborough pie, which is an apple custard pie. Southerners had "no pie but wine jelly, tender and trembling, topped with whipped cream," and Midwesterners stuck to mince and pumpkin.[52]

Fourth of July

In 1893, a local newspaper announced that the annual Fourth of July picnic in Woodland, California, "will be no local affair," as "nearly the whole of the population" of the county was expected to attend.[53] Following the traditions of their ancestors, they probably ate pit-roasted meats set out on rough board tables, mingled with their neighbors, listened to patriotic speeches, and marveled at fireworks displays when the night fell. Similar celebrations were taking place all over the country and had been taking place annually for at least 100 years. As a new century began, however, such events became less and less common. In the Southwest, where barbecue remained an important feature of public gatherings, the tradition seems to have lingered longest. In 1931, for example, readers of the Deming, New Mexico *Headlight* were invited to a Fourth of July gathering in "old town," where five head of cattle were to be barbecued. "Everyone," was invited to "come to the party and have a good time."[54]

In "isolated communities in remote sections of Southern Indiana," too, the "pioneer custom of celebrating Independence Day by a public meeting and barbecue," was still being maintained in the early 1930s. Writer Nelson Algren noted, however, that the menu had changed somewhat over time: "Bear meat and venison, the customary

At a community fair in Pie Town, New Mexico, in 1940, a volunteer slices the cakes and pies while another woman helps herself to some side dishes. (Courtesy of Library of Congress.)

main course, are today supplanted by barbecued beef and mutton. And whereas the pioneers roasted the whole carcass on a spit, today it is roasted in sections."[55]

By 1935, however, a man in rural Kentucky recollected mournfully, "There used to be Fourth of July barbecues, which helped to keep the community spirit strong." By the time he was interviewed, large numbers of young people had moved to cities seeking work and the old festival traditions had begun to die out.[56] By the 1940s, public barbecues, which had sometimes included the roasting of a whole ox, were out of fashion, although fondly remembered by many writers. Smaller towns did continue to hold communal picnics on the Fourth, however. At these events, sometimes called "basket suppers," families brought their own food to eat on blankets. The holiday was not associated with any particular foodstuffs, so baskets were packed with all the traditional picnic staples such as fried chicken, potato salad, cold ham, and cake.

Religious Holidays

In 1939, Jessie Marie De Both published a cookbook titled *Modern Guide to Better Meals* in which she acknowledged the multicultural nature of American foodways. The nation was home to people with diverse food habits who socialized with each other and when they did so, food was often involved. Providing the dates of religious holidays for Roman Catholics, Orthodox Jews, and Greek Orthodox Christians, she noted: "Now and then comes a day, or arrives a guest, in every home, requiring that the thoughtful hostess prepare a special dish or menu in honor of a national custom or in respect for a religious observance."[57] DeBoth offered meatless meals for every month of the year, helping Catholics to observe the custom of not eating meat on Fridays or during the season of Lent.

These meatless meals could also help Jewish homemakers keep kosher by offering dishes that did not mix meat and dairy. Many of DeBoth's suggestions for meals with meat also included dairy, making the book somewhat less useful for Jewish readers than for Catholics. Perhaps as compensation she included a section of traditional Passover recipes such as "Charocis for Sedar" and two kinds of "Filled" or gefilte fish. She also offered the advice that "Proper goose or chicken fat may be used in place of butter."[58] As serious as DeBoth seemed to take dietary laws, she was not above suggesting an all green meal for the celebration of St. Patrick's Day that featured cream of pea soup, shamrock potatoes (mashed potatoes stuffed in a green pepper), spinach, "cloverleaf" rolls, crème de menthe pear salad, and pistachio ice cream.[59]

As any Catholic would have expected, DeBoth's book contained many recipes for fish, as fish was the typical meal for meatless days in Catholic households. The development of fresh freezing brought frozen fish (perhaps too often in the form of fish sticks) to the homes of observant Catholics throughout the country for many years. During the Lenten season of 1941, the U.S. Bureau of Fish and Wildlife offered "suggestions for housewives on fish" in a free fish cookbook that could be acquired through the mail. Because frozen fish "was now less expensive than fresh fish," bureau publicists hoped that homemakers would consider buying it more often, even after Lent as meat prices remained high as a result of wartime demand. Those who preferred to replace their meat with something other than fish would be happy to hear that "supplies are heavier and prices lower than usual" for eggs, a "favorite meat substitute."[60]

For most Americans who adhered to a religious faith, holiday meals involved tradition rather than stricture. Through the 1930s, for example, cookbooks suggested goose as the centerpiece of the Christmas meal as often as they suggested turkey for this role. Goose had been the favorite of English people and their descendants in America for hundreds of years, but turkeys, which served more people, were easier to domesticate, and had a milder flavor and less fat, slowly began to replace them at the holiday table.

Even in meals where turkey was the feast bird, however, the favorite dessert remained the time-honored plum pudding and hard sauce. Thus the Christmas dinner served to the Ninth U.S. Cavalry, stationed in the Philippines in 1900, far from home, included roast turkey, cranberry sauce, green beans and mashed potatoes, and a plum pudding with brandy sauce.[61]

This traditional English festive dessert was usually doused in brandy and set on fire at the moment it was brought to the table. This custom became difficult to observe during the years of Prohibition, when families across America must have been disappointed to learn that "the flavoring of homemade Christmas plum pudding . . . is in violation of the prohibition enforcement law," and puddings were thus "liable to seizure."[62] During the first year of enforcement, however, officials in Boston made an exception so that "mince pies and plum puddings served on the Christmas dinner tables of New England may be seasoned with brandy from the 'individual's supply,'" as long as they were not sold to the public. This "private stock" had presumably been purchased legally before Prohibition laws had gone into effect.[63]

Although it seemed to some that "plum pudding was something you read about in Dickens" rather than eaten in modern America, a survey of "fixed price" or "all you can eat" restaurants in 1932 found that "hard sauce and all, it was a best-seller this past Thanksgiving and Christmas, as it is, indeed, whenever it appears on the menus of the 'all-you-want' restaurants." Perhaps customers felt that because of plum pudding's density, they were getting good value per pound for their dollar.[64]

SPECIAL OCCASIONS

Weddings

By the end of the 19th century it had become traditional to celebrate weddings with a special meal. The form this meal took depended on whether the happy couple and their guests lived in an urban or rural area. In urban areas, the fashion was for a light meal, whereas rural brides and grooms could expect a copious, often outdoor, feast. Wedding announcements for middle class and upper middle class couples often mentioned that a "dainty supper" had followed the ceremony. Alice Bradley's professional guide for caterers, published in 1922, directed that: "It is permissible to serve only a punch or frappe and sweet crackers or cakes, whether the wedding takes place during the day or in the evening." A sample menu for a winter wedding consisted entirely of "coffee with whipped cream. Cherry and nut sandwiches. Wedding cake bonbons."[65] When something more substantial was required, chicken salad was a common choice, often served as part of an all-white, or at least all-pastel meal. Caterer Paul Pierce suggested serving chicken salad in white lettuce cups accompanied by radish roses and white bread and butter sandwiches cut into heart shapes.[66]

When Charles Smith married Emma Koenigheim in San Antonio, Texas, in 1890, however, it was a grand affair, incorporating many of the dishes associated with wedding day meals. The caterer to this event served bouillon with oyster patties, red snapper with sherry sauce, potatoes à la Parisienne, chicken salad, a tenderloin of beef, asparagus in butter, quail with cauliflower, roast duck, a rum omelet, ice cream, and several wedding cakes, as one cake would presumably not have been enough to express their families' joy.[67] Before the meal, the guests gathered to admire the bride's gifts, including diamond jewelry, heaps of silverware, rooms' worth of furniture, and a "check

When radio editor Phyllis Fraser and publisher Bennet Cerf married in 1940, the couple celebrated with a multitier, white-frosted cake, which had become standard wedding fare by the end of the 19th century. (AP Photo.)

from parents of the bride." In Edith Wharton's novel, *The House of Mirth,* a Mrs. Peniston, expressed disdain for a wedding menu that deviated from the norm: "I think it was odd their serving melon before the consommé: a wedding breakfast should always begin with consommé."[68]

For those who married in small towns or rural areas, wedding meals were often set on tables made from boards and barrels to accommodate large crowds. Elinore Pruitt Stewart, a woman who settled in Wyoming in the early 20th century, greeted a newly married couple who had just arrived in her community with a wedding feast at which: "We had a perfectly roasted leg of lamb; we had mint sauce, a pyramid of flaky mashed potatoes, a big dish of new peas, a plate of sponge cake I will be long in forgetting."[69] Zora Neale Hurston portrayed a similar wedding feast in her novel *Their Eyes Were Watching God:* "Janie and Logan got married in Nanny's parlor of a Saturday evening with three cakes and big platters of fried rabbit and chicken.

Everything to eat in abundance."[70] Midwestern author Willa Cather mentioned "six roasted chickens that were to help out at the wedding supper" of her character Claude Wheeler. Wheeler's wedding chickens probably "helped out" at least one ham, some vegetable dishes, and an assortment of cakes and pies.

A farmwoman who attempted to combine urban and rural wedding customs was gently satirized in the novel *Ma Pettengill:* "Then, ho! for the merry wedding breakfast at six thirty A.M.! The wedding breakfast consisted of ham and eggs and champagne. Yes, sir, don't think than Aunt Mollie had overlooked the fashionable drink. Hadn't she been reading all her life about champagne being served at wedding breakfasts?" This celebratory breakfast of ham, eggs, hot sausage, and biscuits served on tables outdoors "was a pretty feast even without the lobster salad," another fashionable wedding dish, "which Aunt Mollie apologized for not having."[71]

Many betrothed couples married at the home of the bride's family, and those who did not frequently had their wedding parties there. In most cases, then, the women of a family, often assisted by neighborhood friends, prepared the food. By 1907, however, one writer noted that in fashionable urban families the cake "is usually ordered of a caterer." For those brides who wanted some hand in its creation, it was also possible to make the cake batter at home and send it out to be baked and iced by professionals.[72] An etiquette manual published in 1921 included the oft-repeated instructions that "At the wedding breakfast or supper, the bride herself makes the first incision in the large frosted cake." This was "the rich black fruit cake which is the time-honored wedding cake," and which "should be made months beforehand and kept in a covered stone crock as it mellows with age. Guests were sent home with precisely measured pieces of cake wrapped up in decorative boxes.[73]

Funerals

Just as Americans greeted the formation of a new family with heavily loaded tables and many cakes, they also piled up food to bid farewell to family and friends. Funeral observances varied according to the religion of the person who had died and what region she had lived in, but across these differences, abundance was a common theme. Whether food was brought to a wake, to a family sitting *shiva,* a funeral supper after the burial, or simply left at the door of the deceased's family, some commonalities can be identified. Casseroles were a popular choice of food as they were easy to transport and to reheat for family meals. In Utah, for example, "funeral potatoes," a potato and cheese casserole, have long been well known as the dish to bring bereaved families.

During the first half of the century, funerals became professionalized as more families took their lost loved ones to funeral homes for burial preparation, and gatherings were held in these somewhat sterile environments. In the process, longstanding food traditions, such as the funeral pie made from raisins, began to fade. There has been something of a resurgence of the association of food and mourning, and some funeral parlors began adding catering facilities to their businesses in the late 20th century.[74]

NOTES

1. Fannie Hurst, *No Food With My Meals* (New York and London: Harper & Brothers Publishers, 1935), p. 9.

2. "Blair," "Domestic Subjects," *The Delineator Magazine* 8, no. 8 (August 1898): 231.

3. Harriet Ross Colquitt, *The Savannah Cook Book* (New York: Farar & Rinehart, 1933), p. 63.

4. Advertisement in the *Venice Vanguard,* July 18, 1919, Los Angeles Public Library Menu Collection digital database.

5. Brae Mar Inn menu, Los Angeles Public Library Menu Collection digital database.

6. Theodore Roosevelt, *Roosevelt's Writings* (New York: The Macmillan Company, 1920), p. 142.

7. Ella Kaiser Carruth "A Card System of Household Accounting," *Journal of Home Economics,* 12, no. 1 (January 1920): 37.

8. Elinore Pruitt Stewart, *Letters of A Woman Homesteader* (Boston: Houghton Mifflin Company, 1914), p. 153.

9. Fremont Rider, ed., *Rider's New York City* (New York: Henry Holt and Company, 1916), p. 20.

10. John A. Jakle and Keith A. Sculle, *Fast Food* (Baltimore: The Johns Hopkins University Press, 1999), p. 36.

11. Jakle and Sculle, *Fast Food,* p. 36.

12. Wanamaker Store Tea Room Daily Menu, 1906, New York Public Library, Miss Frank E. Buttolph American Menu Collection, New York Public Library Rare Books Collection.

13. Siegel Cooper Co. Menu, 1906–1036, Miss Frank E. Buttolph American Menu Collection, New York Public Library Rare Books Collection.

14. R. H. Macy & Co., Five O'clock Tea Menu, 1905–0954, Miss Frank E. Buttolph American Menu Collection, New York Public Library Rare Books Collection.

15. Bullock's Westwood Tea Room Menu, 11, 18, 1938, Los Angeles Public Library Menu Collection digital database.

16. Rider, ed., *Rider's New York City*, p. 26.

17. Rider, ed., *Rider's New York City*, p. 19.

18. Bill of Fare, Edward F. Lang's Ladies' and Gents' Lunchroom Menu, 1900–0451, Miss Frank E. Buttolph American Menu Collection, New York Public Library Rare Books Collection.

19. The Ladies of the Jennings Avenue Methodist Episcopal Church, comp. and eds., *The Twentieth Century Home and Cook Book* (Cleveland, OH, 1903), p. 263.

20. Mrs. G. Edgar Hackney, compiler, *Dining for Moderns* (New York: Published by and for the Benefit of the New York Exchange for Women's Work, 1940), p. 39.

21. Emily Post, "Introduction: The Home Institute of the New York Herald Tribune," *America's Cook Book* (New York: Charles Scribner's Sons, 1937), p. v.

22. The Home Institute of the New York Herald Tribune, *America's Cook Book* (New York: Charles Scribner's Sons, 1937), p. 860.

23. Christine Terhune Herrick, *Consolidated Library of Modern Cooking and Household Recipes* (New York: J. H. Bodmer Company, 1904), p. 41.

24. Alice Bradley, *Cooking for Profits: Catering and Food Service Management* (American School of Home Economics: Chicago, 1925), p. 273.

25. Emily Post, *Etiquette in Society, Business, Politics and at Home* (New York: Funk & Wagnalls Company, 1922), p. 188.

26. Bingham House Hotel Menu, 1899, Miss Frank E. Buttolph American Menu Collection, New York Public Library.

27. Menu of Complimentary Dinner Given by F. H. Putnam to the Red Sox World Champions, 1912. Miss Frank E. Buttolph American Menu Collection, New York Public Library.

28. Mary Lockwood Matthews, *Foods and Cookery and the Care of the House* (Boston: Little, Brown, and Company, 1921), p. 101.

29. Matthews, *Foods and Cookery*, p. 102.

30. Matthews, *Foods and Cookery*, p. 102.

31. Matthews, *Foods and Cookery*, p. 103.

32. Margaret Byington, *Homestead: The Households of a Mill Town* (New York: Russell Sage Foundation, 1910), pp. 64–65.

33. Terhune Herrick, *Consolidated Library of Modern Cooking and Household Recipes*, p. 33.

34. Byington, *Homestead: The Households of a Mill Town*, p. 65.

35. Robert Coit Chapin, *The Standard of Living Among Workingmen's Families in New York City* (New York: Russell Sage Foundation Charities Publication Committee, 1909), p. 312.

36. Maude Hart Lovelace, *Betsy Was a Junior* (New York: Harper Trophy, 1995), p. 138.

37. Paul Bowman Poppenoe, *Modern Marriage* (New York: The Macmillan Company, 1912), p. 2.

38. Margaret Penrose, *The Motor Girls on a Tour* (New York: Cupples & Leon Company, 1910), p. 4.

39. Jakle and Sculle, *Fast Food*, p. 41.

40. Jakle and Sculle, *Fast Food*, pp. 42–43.

41. Eunice Fuller Barnard, "All You Can Eat and What Is Chosen," *New York Times*, February 28, 1932, p. SM11.

42. Fuller Barnard, "All You Can Eat and What Is Chosen," p. SM11.

43. Lauren D. Lyman, "New Planes to Serve Bermuda," *New York Times*, July 26, 1936, p. 207.

44. "'Free' Meals for Bus Tourists," *New York Times*, August 30, 1936, p. XX5.

45. *Journal of Home Economics*, 29, no. 3 (March, 1937): 207.

46. "Airlines' Early Woes with Food Described," *New York Times*, April 26, 1939, p. 4.

47. Menu for Thanksgiving Dinner to Beta Theta Pi Fraternity of Dickinson College, 1892, Miss Frank E. Buttolph Collection of American Menus, New York Public Library.

48. Menu for Thanksgiving Day Dinner, held by Toyo Kisen Kaisha, en route aboard SS Hong Kong Maru, 1900, Miss Frank E. Buttolph Collection of American Menus, New York Public Library.

49. Sue McNamara, Nov. 25, 1931, *Hamilton (Ohio) Evening Journal*, p. 7.

50. Ida Bailey Allen, *Double-quick Cooking*, (New York: M. Barrows and Company, 1943), p. 150.

51. Paul Pierce, *Suppers* (Chicago: Brewer, Barse, & Co., 1907), p. 45.

52. Clementine Paddleford, *How America Eats* (New York: Charles Scribner's Sons, 1960), p. 21.

53. *Woodland (California) Daily Democrat*, June 26, 1893, p. 3.

54. *Deming (New Mexico) Headlight*, July 2, 1931, p. 1.

55. Nelson Algren, *America Eats* (Iowa City: University of Iowa Press, 1992), p. 37.

56. National Child Welfare Committee, *Child Welfare in Kentucky*, (New York: National Child Welfare Committee Incorporated, 1919), p. 132.

57. Jessie Marie DeBoth, *Modern Guide to Better Meals* (Chicago: Printed by Cuneo Press, 1939), p. IV.

58. DeBoth, *Modern Guide to Better Meals*, p. 361.

59. DeBoth, *Modern Guide to Better Meals*, p. 75.

60. "Food News of the Week," *New York Times*, February 28, 1941, p. 15.

61. Christmas Dinner [Held By] Headquarters Ninth U.S. Cavalry Officer's Mess [At] "Manila, P. I.," 1900, Miss Frank E. Buttolph Collection of American Menus, New York Public Library.

62. "Bar Brandied Puddings and Pies at Christmas," *New York Times*, December 4, 1920, p. 12.

63. "May Flavor New England Pies with Private Stock Brandy," *New York Times,* December 6, 1920, p. 17.

64. Fuller Barnard, "All You Can Eat and What Is Chosen," p. SM11.

65. Alice Bradley, *Cooking for Profit* (Chicago: American School of Home Economics, 1922), p. 127.

66. Paul Pierce, *Suppers,* p. 72.

67. "Smith-Koenigheim," *San Antonio Daily Light,* January 6, 1890, p. 7.

68. Edith Wharton, *The House of Mirth* (New York: Charles Scribner's Sons, 1905), p. 173.

69. Elinore Pruitt Stewart, *Letters of A Woman Homesteader* (Boston: Houghton Mifflin Company, 1914), p. 250.

70. Zora Neale Hurston, *Their Eyes Were Watching God* (Urbana-Champaign: The University of Illinois Press, 1991), p. 26.

71. Henry Leon Wilson, *Ma Pettengill* (Garden City, NY: Doubleday, Page & Company, 1919), p. 174.

72. Mrs. Burton Kingsland, *The Book of Weddings* (Garden City, NY: Doubleday, Page & Co., 1907), p. 24.

73. Margaret E. Sangster, *Good Manners for All Occasions* (New York: Cupples & Leon Company, 1921), p. 124.

74. John Leland, "It's My Funeral and I'll Serve Ice Cream if I Want To," *New York Times,* July 20, 2006, http://www.nytimes.com/2006/07/20/fashion/20funeral.html?scp=2&sq=leland%20ice%20cream&st=cse (accessed February 12, 2009).

CHAPTER 5

CONCEPTS OF DIET AND NUTRITION AND FOOD CRISES

Following the tradition of their European ancestors, Americans had long shared an ideal of female and male attractiveness that celebrated the full figure. Plumpness was seen as a sign of economic success, whereas slenderness indicated a lack of means to feed oneself or one's family. In approximately 1910, that ideal changed. Slenderness became the ideal, representative of modernity and echoed in a preference for streamlined design. Extra flesh came to be seen as a sign that a person lacked control of his or her passions and was thus a potentially less productive member of society. In response to this altered ideal, which became especially popular in the 1920s, self-proclaimed experts produced an ocean of advice about how to lose weight. In the same era, the field of human nutrition was born, revealing to researchers, who then shared their knowledge with the public, that there were sensible and foolish ways to eat and that food could make a major contribution to one's health.

In 1913, an advertisement for Magnesurate Compound announced that a "well-known medical practitioner" estimated that approximately 50 percent of the American population suffered from "dyspepsia," a contemporary term for indigestion. The "enormous amount of dyspepsia and its alarming increase from year to year" were both due, the unidentified doctor claimed, to "the fact that we don't live normal lives."[1] Modern society, with its hustle and bustle, had interrupted proper living and eating habits. Sitting at desks in offices and grabbing a quick lunch, as well as dining on "ultra fancy foods," all new habits for ordinary Americans, had taken its toll on the nation's health. The cure was a little bit of "common sense" and a dose of the magic Magnesurate. Advertising claims aside, American lifestyles were undergoing enormous changes at the turn of the century and ideas about food were changing, too. This could certainly be cause for confusion, perhaps even for upset stomachs.

In 1904, a writer in the *New York Times* noted a dizzying number of "diet menus, each one, like the stars differing from the other in glory."[2] The writer then went on to report on the banquet of the Hundred Year Club, whose members did not believe in eating any vegetables, such as potatoes or carrots, that grew below the ground. That same year, another article reported that a Brooklyn man ate only grass and "declared that on that diet he had cured all his ills and risen out of abysmal dyspeptic deeps."[3]

A major change in cookbook publishing also occurred at the beginning of the 20th century. All through the 19th century, cookbooks had tended to take an encyclopedic form, including advice on many matters of the household besides food and had usually offered a section on what was called "invalid cookery," or cooking for the sick. By the early 20th century, cookbooks had become more specialized, focusing just on food and much less often on housekeeping and family matters. In part this was because of changing health practices that saw more middle class Americans using hospitals to care for the terminally and chronically ill. Hospitals, for their part, began to hire dietitians who designed specific menus for different ailments. Also, the wider use of drug-based medicine decreased periods of convalescence. One of the new specialized kinds of cookbooks to appear in this new era was the diet cookbook that recommended a particular way of eating as protective against poor health.

For some, diet advice was a true article of faith, for others just another way to make money off the insecurities of the public. A brief list of dietary supplements advertised between 1890 and 1901 include "cactus blood," which supposedly cured both dyspepsia and eczema; Dr. Epp's cocoa, which "may save us many heavy doctors bills" if we drink it for breakfast; Dr. Pierce's Pleasant Pellets, which could "cure biliousness, sick and bilious headache, dizziness, costiveness, or constipation, sour stomach, loss of appetite, coated tongue," and a host of other ailments; and lactab, a "pure lactic (milk) ferment," which could prevent not only dyspepsia but also old age.[4]

As one journalist reported in 1910, where just "a few years ago an occasional person was met who dieted," now "a sad change has taken place" and "everyone with an instinct for modernity diets."[5] The word diet used as a verb here still meant, as it had in the 19th century, to eat only certain foods with or without a focus on weight loss or gain. Restricting one's diet had become so fashionable, this writer argued, that the only way to have a dinner party was for each guest to bring raw ingredients and the host to provide "an alcohol lamp apiece" for cooking it. A humorous column in an Iowa newspaper noted: "One of the late schemes is to adopt a fruit diet. The advocates of this claim that fruit was the original diet of man," and therefore the only proper food. Another food "'cult' swears by raw food," and yet another "come[s] with cooked food already prepared and some of it predigested."[6] This last comment was probably a reference to the theories of Horace Fletcher, who advocated chewing each mouthful of food 32 times for healthy digestion.

FLETCHERISM

Horace Fletcher was a self-proclaimed diet expert born in Massachusetts in 1849. Although he did not have advanced scientific training, he conducted experiments in the laboratories of some of the world's most well-respected universities to test his theories of diet. Fletcher believed that most people wasted food by not chewing enough before swallowing. According to Fletcher, human beings could subsist on much less food than the typical American ate by simply chewing it more. This earned him the nickname "the Great Masticator." If they would "fletcherize" their food, eaters would find that "the mouth becomes a filter . . . for protecting the alimentary canal from straining or poisoning."[7] But chewing was not enough, Fletcher explained. The eater should always be in a good mood. According to his research, "cheerfulness is as important as chewing; and if persons cannot be cheerful during a meal they had better not eat." Claiming that ill humor during mealtime led directly to indigestion, Fletcher begged his readers, "don't chew anything when you are mad or when you are sad, but only when you are glad you are alive."[8]

The positive spirit of Fletcher's diet fit well with a cultural focus on vigor and innovation and became popular among social and cultural leaders of the day. President Theodore Roosevelt and writer Mark Twain both tried the diet and even J. H. Kellogg, one of the most famous diet reformers of the 19th century, practiced fletcherism and publicly endorsed Fletcher's theories. While the fad for "munching parties" faded quickly, one component of Fletcher's dietary philosophy did have lasting impact. Because he ate less than the ordinary American, Fletcher consumed less protein than what was recommended by experts of the era. That he was able to maintain strength and health on a lower protein diet intrigued contemporary experts, who used some of his ideas to redesign emergency rations for the U.S. Army.[9]

A less widely adopted feature of Fletcher's philosophy was his interest in bodily excretions as evidence of the good and bad in diet. Although many were happy to at least try chewing their food and only eating while cheerful, few wished to examine their own excretions after doing so. If they had chosen to, Fletcher assured them that those with a good diet would find their excreta "inoffensive," or odorless.

THE DR. HAY DIET

Those who did not find fletcherizing to their taste could turn to a contemporary, William Howard Hay, for another new approach to food and eating. Hay, born in 1866 in New York, practiced as a traditional physician at the beginning of his career but by 1932 was "one of the country's best-known dietary advisors." He believed that some foods were alkali forming and some acid forming, meaning that they produced either acid or alkali conditions in the stomach.[10] When alkali and acid-forming foods were mixed in one meal, or when too much acid-forming food was consumed, he claimed the result was illness. This led to a complex calculus of what kinds of food could be eaten together. In *Health Via Food*, Hay advocated keeping proteins and carbohydrates separate, using almost no milk, and eating only a small amount of meat, making vegetables and fruits the main foodstuffs. Declaring that "we in America are the sickest nation on the face of the whole earth," Hay encouraged readers to change their way of eating by beginning with a fast during which nothing was consumed but orange juice.[11]

Hay was appointed Health Director of the Sun-Diet Sanatorium in East Aurora, New York, in 1927. Oliver Cabana, a wealthy businessman with unusual views on diet and health, had opened the sanatorium. Cabana advocated a mostly vegetarian diet and offered sun treatments—either natural or artificial "with the aid of the very latest and finest equipment"—to paying guests of the sanatorium.[12]

Hay offered the public not just model menus, which he described as "a compromise between conventional habit in eating and the ideal diet," but also a new way of thinking about food. He proposed that "this old world, from our individual viewpoint, will not be such a very bad place to spend a long life," once "we have learned to look on food as replacement material, not something to tickle the palate."[13] Like the first generation of trained nutritionists who were his contemporaries, Hay wanted people to think of food as fuel. His advice differed from nutritionists, however, because it wasn't based on laboratory research, but rather on his own notions about food and on anecdotal evidence. A further difference was that nutritionists also studied palatability—whether people liked to eat a particular food—in order to help people want to eat the foods that were good for them. Hay seems to have considered taste a distraction.

Following Hay's diet, a person could expect to eat quite differently from the great majority of Americans. In general, Hay did not approve of breakfast as a meal. His mentor and patron, Oliver Cabana, joyfully declared that he himself had not had breakfast in "over twenty-five years." Lest readers doubt him, he explained, "When I tell you that I eat no breakfast, I mean that I take ABSOLUTELY NOTHING. I am entirely independent of the breakfast room, the cook, the waitresses, everything and everybody that has to do with eating. When I walk out of my room in the morning I keep right on going until I am out of the house and down to business."[14]

If breakfast must be eaten, Hay advised, "The day is best started with a fruit breakfast." Some might also have a glass or two of raw milk, but Hay was as ambivalent about milk as he was about breakfast itself: "If milk is taken at all, [breakfast] is the best meal at which to take it." Because the ideal diet did not include breakfast, it also omitted milk.[15] He admitted that if the reader was "accustomed to a hot and concentrated breakfast this will leave you feeling that you have had no breakfast at all." If one would "stick to it until it becomes customary," however, Hay promised new vigor and "great activity."[16]

A typical lunch was "Pea puree; steamed squash; steamed chicory; Salad: Lettuce, Cabbage and raisin, Dressing 5 [whipped cream, oil, honey]; Dessert: Dates and Cream." The inclusion of dessert was a grudging concession to popular habits, as Hay believed that end-of-the-meal sweets "represent excess, a mere catering to the palate to leave it pleased at the end of a perhaps too full meal." If the diner must have dessert, it had better be fresh fruit and, if the meal had contained starch, that fruit had better not be acid. Why cream was acceptable when milk was not, Hay did not explain.

For those who, as Hay wrote, "have no religious or ethical scruples against the use of animal corpses as food," he recommended eating meat no more than twice a week.[17] Instead, he suggested dishes such as "cream of mushroom soup; vegetable meat loaf; steamed spinach and baked eggplant" followed by a salad of lettuce, cabbage, and celery dressed with mayonnaise.[18] Those who did not have the willpower to resist dessert could indulge in applesauce, steamed figs, or perhaps a decadent bowl of "grape gelatine."

A contemporary critic of fad diets dismissed Hay's book as "a hodgepodge of misinformation that has received the condemnation it deserves from every authoritative medical publication that has bothered to say anything about it."[19] What Hay did not seem to understand, this critic explained, was that "(1) few foods are either wholly protein or wholly carbohydrate in composition, (2) that the stomach is *always* acid, and (3) that digestion is carried on not only in the mouth and stomach, but in the intestinal tract as well."[20] In other words, the body is well equipped to digest both alkali and acid foods, and it would be impossible to separate out the two anyway.

Undeterred by the simple facts of biology, the Defensive Diet League, lead by G. E. Harter and his wife Sunolia Vaughn Harter, adopted some of Hay's ideas to advocate the "80/20 diet" described in the *80/20 Cook Book and Food Manual*. Followers of this diet balanced their meals to include 20 percent acid and 80 percent alkali. The Defensive Diet League appears to have been a for-profit enterprise, selling "D-D.L." ingredients that were required for making many of the recipes included in the *80/20 Cook Book*. Among these ingredients, which the Harters promised readers would find in local stores, were D-D.L. sugar, D-D.L. powdered soups, and D-D.L. canned fruits. D-D.L. sugar was the only sugar allowed to 80/20 dieters, who could otherwise turn only to maple syrup and honey for sweeteners. The 80/20 diet included very little meat, replacing the traditional meat main course with fish or a raw vegetable loaf composed of grated vegetables mixed with melted butter and chilled. Breakfasts always included both fruit and milk; lunches were very light, typically no more than some cottage cheese and fruit or a bowl of soup. The influence of such diets seems to have spread most quickly to breakfast, which became a much smaller meal than it had been during the 19th century. One character in a novel published in 1913, for example, ate a "wise and cautious breakfast of fruit and cereal and toast and coffee."[21]

VEGETARIAN DIETS

Practiced by small groups and individuals over the course of the 19th century, vegetarianism became somewhat more common at the turn of the century. Writing in a popular women's magazine in 1897, Grace Peckham Murray, a physician, announced: "The subject of vegetarianism is coming more and more to the front and is no longer treated with ridicule by thoughtful people."[22] She even offered the readers some sample menus so that they could try a day or two of vegetarian living for themselves. Murray's menus appear to bring together a collection of side dishes from carnivorous cookbooks rather than considering vegetables on their own merits. For example, lunch brought together "cream soup, celery, olives, macaroni tomato sauce, browned sweet potatoes, boiled onions, rice croquettes [with] sweet sauce, lettuce salad, crackers and cheese," followed by "fairy pudding with yellow sauce, fruit, coffee." Quantity was perhaps supposed to make up for the quality presumed to lack when meat was missing.

Vegetarianism was associated in the early years of the 20th century with many special diet plans. Sanitaria were established where those who suffered from a variety of ailments could go in search of a rest and diet cure and many of these served mostly vegetarian fare, thereby no doubt keeping their operating costs low. *The Los Angeles Times* cookbook of 1905 included a recipe for celery soup from the Esperanza Sanatorium, noting that it was "for vegetarians" and also "very good."[23] Another person who contributed to the cookbook offered two versions of "Vegetarian Salad," suggesting that meatlessness was becoming more acceptable in mainstream food ways and also that the typical salad had some kind of meat in it.[24]

While vegetarianism as a lifestyle was very popular in England at the turn of the century, it was much less so in America. As the editor of a New York City vegetarian magazine noted sadly in 1895, "London, England, has nearly fifty strictly vegetarian restaurants. The great city of New York, the second city in the world, has one small restaurant where food uncontaminated by dead animals can be obtained."[25] A year earlier, a small group of students at the University of Chicago had "received the intellectual revelation that it is impossible to be moral beings and carnivorous animals at the same instant" and consequently formed a vegetarian eating club, where members paid $2.50 a week for "unique and beautiful menus."[26] Nonetheless, the vegetarian community in America remained so small that a long-running journal, the Vegetarian and Fruitarian had to serve both those who ate vegetables and fruit and those who ate only fruit. A special column dedicated to raw food addressed the anticooking crowd and frequent attacks on the eating of eggs and milk recognized a vegan audience. For those too depressed by America's mania for meat, vegetarians formed several colonies, one in Chiriqui, Panama, where meat was forbidden and clothing was optional.

During the food crises of the world wars and the Great Depression, when meat was in short supply, many vegetarian, and "meat-less" recipes were published to help Americans deal with shortages of their beloved staple food. Thetta Quay Franks who wrote *Daily Menus for*

War Service in 1918 suggested that the shortage of meat might last beyond the war and that it would be good to be ready for a meatless future. She noted: "Meat is the most expensive food and is rapidly rising in price because there is not enough to supply the demand." Therefore, "It may be wise for us to know in time that we can be well fed and healthy without meat."[27] U.S. ration cards allowed for two-and-one-half pounds of meat per person per week, which Franks worked out to four ounces per meal. With such small portions, she may have reasoned, meat might not be missed at all. Meatless Americans who still wanted to use the carnivore's terminology could feast on "Boston Roast," a mixture of equal parts mashed kidney beans and cheese rolled up, roasted, and basted with butter.[28] Those who wanted to use the opportunity of wartime meatless Tuesday to experiment might like to try curried bananas with rice.[29]

One vegetarian advocate saw the hardship of the Great Depression as a perfect opportunity for government-sponsored vegetarianism. She charged that charity as currently practiced was "a menace—an insult." Typical supplies of "white bread, salt pork, and grease canned vegetables" were "all deficient, inferior foods." Instead, relief agencies should provide vegetables like potatoes and carrots, whole grains, brown sugar, and cooking oil and then teach the destitute some proper vegetarian cooking. Worst of all was when relief included canned meats, or "salted and embalmed antediluvian canned cadaver," which she imagined "only makes life more miserable for the poor and adds insult to injury."[30]

TOO FAT? TOO THIN?

During the first 50 years of the 20th century, perceptions of health and beauty altered radically, changing the way that ordinary people approached their mirrors and wielded their forks. From a commonly shared admiration of plumpness as indicative of health, American aesthetics shifted to favor slenderness. Toned and visible muscles, once a mark of low social status, became celebrated as a symbol of virility in men. Similarly, curveless female bodies, once thought to indicate poverty and hunger, were now favored by fashion. This change happened rather drastically in the 1920s, as novelist Fannie Hurst recalled: "Suddenly . . . the biology of my entire sisterhood seemed to have undergone an evolution. Female silhouettes began to take on the concavity of the letter C . . . The bust measurements of the potential and actual mothers of the race dropped to the proportions of their

At the end of the 19th century, it was still considered aesthetically pleasing for women to be plump. This advertisement for Fat-ten-u offers those without curves a dietary supplement to attain them. (Courtesy of Library of Congress.)

young sons and brothers. The old, well-nourished ideal of the Venus de Milo became a lummox."[31]

The new aesthetic did not become dominant overnight, however, and advertisements for dietary supplements to fatten one up ran alongside those for supplements to slim one down. In one 1896 edition of the *Delineator,* a popular women's magazine, readers could find both an advertisement for "Dr. Edison's obesity reducing compound," and, a few pages later, an invitation to "Get Fat by using Loring's Fat-ten-u and Corpula Foods." Dr. Edison announced it was "Time to Be Thin!" and included a testimonial from a woman who "restored [her] waist line and bust line, long obscured in fat." Now, she had "no dread of summer." Since the fashions of 1896 revealed very little of the body, it may be that the unnamed woman was looking forward to carrying less weight in the summer heat rather than to exposing more flesh. For its part, Loring's formula promised to "make the thin plump and comely" and could also "impart VIM to the debilitated." The Loring's ad, too, had a seasonal theme: noting that "Used during the early Summer these foods Fortify the System Against the dangers of hot weather."[32]

For those who wished to use a dietary route to plump comeliness, Bertha Johnston, the author of *Eat and Grow Slender* had another volume, *Eat and Grow Fat*. The book was addressed to "those who, whether or not they are justified in the thought, feel that they are 'too thin,' and therefore naturally desire to 'lay on' more adipose tissue, if that be possible."[33] Johnston seemed at every turn to doubt the real necessity of her own book, suggesting that there was no medical reason to put on weight, and that the whole trouble was really in the mind. For the person "who knows himself to be ultra lean, lank, bony, or has memories of having been nicknamed 'skinny' by the heartless companions of his boyhood, the knowledge is a cause of genuine anguish of spirit (out of proportion perhaps, to its relative importance)."[34] Luckily for the anguished skinny person, it was much easier to put weight on than to take it off and Johnston's suggested menus were quite appetizing. A breakfast to be eaten in September, for example, consisted of "plums, stewed or fresh; wheatena; hamburg steak on toast, lyonnaise potatoes."[35] When dieting to gain weight, one should take real cream in one's coffee and of course "those of the lean fraternity who have a sweet tooth are fortunate (especially if they have a fat purse), for sugar and candy should form part of their diet."[36] Another book recommended that the underweight enjoy ice cream or a milkshake every day for a mid-afternoon snack.[37] A guide to calorie consciousness in a 1926 household manual recommended a diet of just over 1,000 calories for "a woman who wishes to reduce," and a diet of about 3,000 calories per day for "the woman who wishes to put on weight," with the difference mostly taking the form of fats. The woman who wanted to gain weight, for example was invited to enjoy both "creamy rice pudding" and "chocolate with whipped cream" at lunch after she had consumed some cream soup and an omelet with bacon.[38]

By the 1930s, however, slenderness was the cultural ideal, and the Sears Roebuck catalog offered such dietary aids as Hollywood 18 Salts: "The reducing method used by the movie stars who must keep their lovely, slim figures." Yet the look of health was still considered attractive as an advertisement for Kelp-a-Malt urged readers, "Don't Stay Skinny and Unattractive because your system lacks essential Vitamin B and Iron." The advertisement featured a curvaceous woman in a swimsuit regarded by two men, one of whom said to the other, "You'd never believe she was skinny a few months ago."[39] Most of the slimming salts and teas marketed were nothing more than diuretics or laxatives either of which, if taken too frequently, was not good for digestive health. Some of the laxatives marketed during the 1920s and 1930s were Germania Herb Tea; Manikin Tea; Elfin Fat Reducing Gum Drops; Slends Reducing Gum; and Figuroids.[40] Diet pills that used thyroid to speed up metabolism included Faid, Silph Chewing Gum, PHY-thy-rin, Rengo, Kellogg's Safe Fat Reducer, and San-Gri-Na.[41]

Because movies popularized the new aesthetic, the designers of diets and makers of diet supplements often tried to associate their products with Hollywood and the movie stars who worked there. As Fannie Hurst noted in 1935: "More and more, today's standards of American Beauty are being set up and authorized by the bizarre little so-called civilization known as Hollywood, home of the eighteen-day diet, the orange juice diet, the skimmed-milk-and-baked-potato, the liquid bread, the thyrodic bath salt, the paraffin sweat, the holy-rolling machine, the pugilistic massage, and almost every reduction fad known to this tormented year of our Lord."[42]

The Hollywood Eighteen Day Diet, to which Hurst referred, was a weight loss plan of "unusual popularity" that, according to one writer, "swept the country like a plague during the 1920s."[43] The Hollywood Eighteen Day Diet provided 18 days of menus to be followed strictly. There was little variation within the menus and dieters essentially lived on grapefruit and Melba toast, losing weight through drastically lowering their calorie intake. The diet reached a wide audience because the powerful California citrus industry promoted it as did the Cubbison Cracker Company of Los Angeles, which manufactured Melba toast.[44] The diet was so popular that some restaurants added it to their menus, and "it was possible to enter a restaurant and order the luncheon for the twelfth day or the dinner for the seventeenth day, depending on what point in the diet had been reached."[45]

A doctor, William Engel, "accidentally" set off a diet craze that had people eating only lamb chops and pineapple, when he was asked by "one of Hollywood's leading actresses . . . to relieve her of forty pounds in four weeks." He told her that this was a dangerous thing to attempt, to which she replied, "What does it matter? If I am not forty pounds lighter when I face the cameras next month, they'll turn me out to starve to death anyway." He asked what her favorite foods were and when she "picked lamb chops and pineapple," he told her to eat nothing but this except for a normal breakfast. As she found herself restricted, she soon ate less and less of her favorites and so lost weight fast. This started a craze that Engel reported was "disastrous" for the health of many who tried it in the attempt to look like a glamorous actress.[46]

In 1940, socialite and actress Mariposa Hayes attempted to capital-
ize on the ordinary woman's desire to look like a movie star when she
published the *Hollywood Glamour Cook Book*. In this lively guide to
"glamorizing" through diet, Hayes borrowed from nutrition science
and fad diets alike, making up her own rules along the way. Advocating liberal use of herbs, Hayes apparently had a mail order business
selling the "Hollywood Herb Kit," which readers could order from
Mariposa herself in Miami. Such specialty herbs as "Mermaid Gelo"
and "Glamour Flour," available by mail, were, after all, not likely to
be found in local groceries. Another essential ingredient in the Hollywood Glamour diet was goat's milk. Readers would find goat's milk
expensive, Hayes acknowledged, but offered them this brief verse as a
lesson in supply and demand:

> The reason goat's milk is so high
> They need more 'Glamour Girls' to buy;
> But when it's bought in quantity,
> the price will drop enormously.
> So order goat's milk twice a week
> and keep your beauty at its peak.[47]

Although advising readers to avoid beef and to only eat whole
grains, the Hollywood Glamour diet was far from joyless. Hayes listed
all of the "herbs" to be found in liquor, thereby justifying its use.
Borrowing the acid/alkali concept from the Dr. Hays diet, she acknowledged that "nearly every alcoholic drink is very acid forming
and we must protect Miss Glamour from 'acidosis.'" Hayes suggested
"a secret hint from Hollywood," which was to drink Celestine mineral water with cocktails. With mineral water and herbs, a cocktail was
practically a health drink:

> Good Old Tom Gin will help the most
> With Canapes and soy bean toast
> To play the part of perfect host
> At cocktail time from coast to coast
> So mix it well with Celestine
> And bits of Mint still young and green.
> A dash of sweet—say here's a treat
> That any guest will call complete![48]

Mariposa even offered menus based on astrology, enthusing, "Just
think of it, we are going to let the Planets give you a short-cut to

Health and Beauty! Can you think of a more thrilling way?" A sample menu for a Scorpio's dinner on a Saturday was the following: "Soup, Caraway Seed, minced parsley, Baked soy macaroni (no tomato), vegetable flour rolls, Steamed broccoli, lemon butter sauce, Grated tender raw kohlrabi and green dill leaves, Hollywood French dressing, Butterscotch coffee ice cream, chocolate oatmeal raisin cookies, Hollywood cup or Figco, raw sugar, cream."[49]

As more people grew interested in losing weight, diet books became a lucrative market. An appropriately slim volume titled *Eat and Grow Slender,* published even before weight loss diets were at their peak of popularity, acknowledged that "There are few who want to be 'fat' as the small boy expresses it. It is bad enough to be 'stout' to employ the euphemism used by one's friends, when they wish to spare our feelings."[50] This guide, like many others to come later, mixed real science with quackery to produce a weight loss plan. Readers were advised that "the over-fat must abstain from the fats and carbo-hydrates which are fat producing," and get lots of exercise, which seems reasonable enough, but the book also advised deep breaths before sleeping, "to supply the blood with an ample amount of oxygen, to promote the burning of surplus fat," advice of questionable value. Followers of this diet were also given the unscientific command to eat at each meal "only what will fill an ordinary tea-cup."[51]

DISCOVERY OF VITAMINS

At the same time that the market in diets that largely traded on unproven theories was thriving, scientists were actually discovering what are now the cornerstones of nutritional science and beginning to know the human body in its relation to food as it had never been known before. These researchers looked at food in terms of its chemical components. And as word of their discoveries filtered out from the laboratories, amateur dietitians and charlatans alike seized on poorly understood elements to design ideal diets and to sell these to the public. Inundated with information about food and the body, Americans might well have had a hard time knowing what to eat.

"Be Happy, Stop Worrying," a 1913 newspaper headline encouraged culinarily confused readers. The U.S. Department of Agriculture (USDA) had issued a "warning against freak diets" and suggested that Americans use their own traditions as their dietary guide.[52] Letters from citizens perplexed by diet advice from experts of more and less respectable credentials had prompted Secretary of Agriculture David

Houston to issue a call for calm. Instead of following fads such as the recently popular raw food diet, Huston's advice was to "eat with moderation a diet made up of clean wholesome ordinary foods well prepared in the usual way."

Although it was "true enough many of the 'food experts' are fakers," and much contemporary wisdom "little more than folklore," at least one critic objected to the vagueness of Houston's advice.[53] What was "ordinary" food? What was the "usual way" to prepare it? And who could tell what qualified as a moderate diet? To combat the storm of misinformation, there was a need for facts arrived at scientifically. And these facts were, the critic was relieved to say, increasingly available. Despite the cheerful conservatism of the secretary of agriculture, "it is too late now to stem the tide of progress in dietetic reform." In the last years of the 19th and the first of the 20th century, scientists were asking more questions and getting more answers about food than ever before.

In 1915, Albert S. Gray, a doctor who wrote for the popular press, explained that "two new words have recently been added to our vocabulary, 'hormones' by Starling in 1906 and 'vitamines' by Funk in 1912."[54] An understanding of how the human body functioned and how it processed food had altered dramatically since the turn of the century. Scientists had suspected the existence of what came to be known first as "vitamines" and then vitamins, but they had not been able to isolate them in the laboratory (and thereby claim proof of their existence) until the 1910s. Vitamins were understood to be substances that were essential to health and that had to be supplied through food. Absence of these substances in a diet results in specific illnesses, such as scurvy, beriberi, and pellagra.

A Polish scientist, Casimir Funk, coined the term *vitamine* in 1912, combining the term *vita*, which means "life," with "amine" because he thought, not quite correctly, that the substances he was studying were amino acids. Many researchers disliked the term, but it stuck, nonetheless. In 1913, American biochemist Elmer McCollum was able to isolate and thus "discover" vitamin A and vitamin B. Isolation and also synthesis of other vitamins soon followed and, by 1940, nutritionists had basic knowledge of the essential vitamins and had begun to understand the role they played in maintaining human health. Nonetheless, a writer in 1942 thought it necessary to tell her readers that the word was "pronounced vi-tah-min," suggesting that many people were still unaware of this significant discovery.[55]

Experiments to determine the function of vitamins involved both chemical analysis and use of laboratory animals. Most experiments used rats because they have metabolisms similar to humans. To understand the functions of vitamin C, however, guinea pigs had to be used because rats actually synthesize this vitamin naturally and thus do not need to get it through their diets. Vitamin experiments typically involved feeding one group of rats or guinea pigs a diet devoid of the vitamin under study and a control group a normal diet. Photographs taken as part of these early studies show experimental rodents of dramatically different appearances as a result of the presence or absence of a particular vitamin in their diet.

The USDA, which had been funding research in nutrition since 1883, opened an office of Home Economics in 1915 to organize research in human nutrition, food science, and dietetics, as well as other topics related to domestic life and labor. Nutrition is the study of how the chemical makeup of foods affects the human body; food scientists study how foods react to various processes such as freezing or baking; and dietetics is the study of connections among food, illness, and health.

The office, which was to become the Bureau of Home Economics in 1923, oversaw research in a wide range of subjects including vitamins and other elements of nutrition. Government-employed home economists produced thousands of free bulletins for Americans explaining basic nutrition and suggesting menus and recipes to help families achieve healthy diets. State universities and agricultural extension services (originally developed to bring up-to-date agricultural knowledge to farmers) also began to publish information on human nutrition and to include the topic in their outreach programs. The goal of the bulletins was typically to help families make the most of what was available to them, rather than to introduce them to new foodstuffs. This fit well with the larger goal of the USDA and state agricultural departments to support American agriculture. Sometimes, when agricultural scientists thought it might be good for American farmers to try a new crop, government food scientists helped them out by finding ways to use the new crop in recipes.

Extension agents working in nutrition research and outreach were also able to tackle the problem of pellagra, which was common in southern communities, where diets tended to be low in niacin. Pellagra sufferers, who were among the poorest farmers in rural areas, experienced weakness, stomach disorders, mouth sores, and skin problems, which made it difficult for them to work. Extension programs that taught them to eat niacin-rich foods such as greens, milk, and lean meats largely eliminated pellagra as a problem in communities where it had once been endemic.

POPULAR EDUCATION IN NUTRITION

Extension agents and bulletin writers hoped to convince ordinary Americans to think about food in terms of units and balance. Each meal was a unit in the family's diet and each dish a unit in a meal. Each food the family ate was composed of units of protein, vitamin, and minerals that should all be kept in balance for optimum health. Thus each meal should be carefully composed to provide the highest possible "food value." If one meal of the day provided high value of one component, then the other two meals could offer less of it. An example of this might be that a family having meat, which is a good source of iron, for dinner would not need large quantities of other iron-rich foods for breakfast or lunch. The term *recommended daily allowances* was coined by Bureau of Home Economics nutritionist Hazel Stiebeling in the 1930s, but the concept existed earlier. Nutritionists encouraged home cooks to think of the family diet mathematically rather than emotionally or aesthetically. What mattered most was the chemical nature of the meal. Because this was such a new way to think about food, nutritionists and dietitians used a wide range of outlets, including bulletins produced by state agencies and columns in women's magazines, to share their science with consumers.

In 1921, nutritionist Walter Hollis Eddy noted that the basic diet of the American people was "a meat, potato and cereal diet," notably lacking in both dairy and green vegetables and therefore nutritionally deficient. Most Americans considered salads "a foreign affectation," and "too little attention has been paid to the value of eggs, milk and cheese."[56] Respected food experts such as Sarah Tyson Rorer had based recommendations, not on scientific research but rather on personal experience. Noting in 1907 that "we are at present, to be sure, in a great confusion over the right and wrong of the food question," Rorer, a successful cookbook author, claimed the right to give advice because "I have practiced certain dietary theories on myself and children, as well as on those suffering from disease, who are now, like myself, well from the beginning to the end of the year."[57] The diets she recommended relied on updated, but still unscientific, versions of ancient theories of body chemistry in which blood and lymph and temperature all played important roles. Rorer believed, for example, that nutritional needs changed with climate: "In cold climates we increase the carbonaceous foods, fats, sugars and starches, to keep up the bodily fires. In warmer climates we decrease both the nitrogenous and carbonaceous foods and add fruits and succulent green vegetables to keep the body cool."[58] In reality, although foodways may reflect different regional lifestyles, the basic food needs of the human body are consistent across the globe and throughout the year. Given that Americans ate an unbalanced diet and encountered unscientific advice about food, the nutritionists who began their work in the 1910s and 1920s had much to do.

An early attempt to share nutritional science with the public was made at the World Columbian Exposition in Chicago in 1893. There, biochemist Ellen Swallow Richards and social reformer Mary Hinman Abel set up a kitchen in which to model new ideas about food and cooking. They called it the Rumford kitchen after Benjamin Thompson, Count Rumford, a pioneer food scientist who died in 1814. The kitchen served visitors simple, wholesome meals that were meant to demonstrate how good nutrition could be achieved with very low cost. Because of the positive response from the public, a set of pamphlets handed out at the Exposition were later published together as the Rumford kitchen leaflets. For those who had not been able to visit the kitchen in Chicago, the wisdom of the leading nutritionists was made available. The leaflets explained such important topics as "The Place of Fats in Nutrition," "The Prophylactic and Therapeutic Value of Food," and how to obtain "Good Food for Little Money."[59]

By the early 1920s, more Americans would have been familiar with the term *vitamin*, but few knew enough about these substances to act wisely on their knowledge. A one-act play written in 1928 as part of a series on rural life dramatized the general ignorance of nutrition. In the play, *Balanced Diet*, a mother who has been taking a home reading course in nutrition and a daughter who has been studying the subject in college attempt to change the eating habits of the family patriarch. Worrying that a diet of fried starches has been making him dyspeptic, the two women serve him a lighter lunch of soup, peas, and ham baked with potatoes in a fireless cooker. "Pa" objects strenuously, especially when his daughter tells him that his traditional meals have lacked vitamins. "Vitamins"— Pa exclaims, "What's vitamins? I've lived so fur without havin' tasted sech stuff. Next thing you'll be givin' me a dish o' vitamins." When his daughter attempts to explain that vitamins are in everything that he has been eating, he continues to misunderstand, accusing her and her mother of "puttin' more medicine in my food!"[60]

To help people like this fictional farmer understand the nature of vitamins and the basics of human nutrition, C. Houston Goudiss, an "intelligent populizer of science," published *Eating Vitamines*, a guide for "How to Know and Prepare Foods That Supply These Invisible Life-guards" in 1922.[61] This "first household guide to be offered the

American homemaker," on the subject of vitamins credited Ernest McCollum with discovering "how to keep the human family from starving on a full stomach," and offered the secret to good health: "drink milk; eat leaf vegetables."[62] Both milk and leafy green vegetables contain vitamins essential to good nutrition, and both had been only marginally featured in the traditional American diet. To feed her family well, Goudiss explained that "the woman who has the menu making in hand" needed to consider "eight items" for each meal. These were "the quantity of food eaten; the proportions of protein, fats, carbohydrates, vitamines, mineral salts, cellulose ; and the variety of foodstuffs included in the bill of fare."[63] To help with this complicated process, Goudiss supplied menus and "recipes rich in vitamins." Cream soups won his approval because they included both vegetables and milk, two good sources of essential vitamins. Goudiss offered a few meat recipes, but he also encouraged readers to eat fish and provided a much larger chapter on meat substitutes, reflecting a shared sense among nutritionists of the era that Americans ate more meat than was good for them and that a more diverse diet would improve national nutrition.

A cookbook published in 1943, however, cautioned home cooks not to go too far with their new knowledge. Physician Leona Beyer and her co-author Edith Green offered homemakers useful advice about how to understand and use nutritional science to feed their families but warned them that making "the meal time a pleasure . . . means doing the work on dietetics in the kitchen, not at the table." In other words, mothers should make healthy meals but not talk about them. Another cookbook author agreed "nutrition has to be sold to the family, but not by strong-arm methods." Although mothers could be trusted to find out what was healthy and eat it, "Men and children will not eat food because it is 'good for them'—unless they like it!" The trick was to make nutritious food tasty and "above all—don't talk about it!"[64]

In 1942, Americans got a gory but inspiring lesson in nutrition when three members of the American Air Force were rescued after more than a month at sea on a raft. Shot down and left to drift without compass, rudder, or food, the three subsisted on fish they caught. As described in a pamphlet published by the American Federation of Labor, "Day after day, hunger gnawed at their stomachs," until "Aldrich, the pilot, had a brilliant idea. Some time before he had read or heard something about nutrition and vitamins. He vaguely recalled that liver eaten raw could supply the body with practically all the vitamins needed for health," so he commenced killing albatrosses and feeding himself and comrades on the bird's liver. Because the liver was a good source of vitamin C, the castaways avoided scurvy, a common ailment among sailors.[65]

COUNTING CALORIES

Simultaneous to the discovery of vitamins, the term *calorie* entered common usage, as Wilbur Atwater, a chemist who studied food, published his findings on how the body used up food energy. Atwater used a contraption called a calorimeter to perform experiments. The calorimeter was a large, roomlike box in which human study subjects performed various physical tasks while machinery calculated the amount of energy expended by keeping track of how much they were breathing. Some activities performed inside the calorimeter for the sake of research were standing, sitting, sleeping, studying for college exams, and ironing.

As it became clear that burning, or using up, calories had something to do with weight loss, Americans began counting calories in ways that did not always make scientific sense. Rather than strategizing ways to burn off excess calories, the ordinary person who worried about weight was more likely to try to limit calorie intake. What one did not "eat one would not" have to burn. Fannie Hurst called calorie counting "that strange branch of lower mathematics"[66] and author Carl Malmberg noted, "Many diet books tend to oversimplify the problem by stating that all that is necessary is a reduction in the number of calories in one's food." Following this advice, Malmberg worried, "is inviting disaster just as surely as one who crosses a crowded street against a red light."[67] Important nutrients might easily be lost through this method of dieting. Diet book author and physician William Engel wrote colorfully: "Fat is a calorie that has not lived. It is frustrated power—born to magnetize a woman's charm, but doomed by plenty to waste itself upon her bulging hip. Poor calorie! Its mistress ate not wisely but too well when, wisely, she might have feasted like the gods and risen like a goddess lovely to behold."[68]

The logic of reducing weight by reducing calories seemed just too obvious to too many people. Thus diets like the Hollywood Eighteen Day diet with its very limited number of calories per day became popular. It did not help the cause of public understanding that nutritionists themselves did not seem to agree on the optimal number of calories to consume each day. Appropriately but confusingly, different numbers were recommended for people of different genders, ages, and occupations and there were no set numbers even within the different categories. The dieting public, lacking patience, had a tendency to search out the lowest number and aim for that, thinking of calories as something bad rather than as the fuel for physiological functioning.

In 1926, when Christine Terhune Herrick set out to update her mother's popular cookbook and household management guide, *Common Sense in the Household,* she noted that "the calorie in its meaning as a unit of measure was not popularly recognized when" the book first appeared in 1871. Now, however, "with an increase in knowledge of food values in relation to the proper nourishment of the body, the importance became apparent of understanding the number of calories contained in specific articles of diet." Mothers preparing family meals must now take into consideration the caloric needs of each member of the family, values that were bound to vary. According to "the latest authorities upon nutrition," children ages two to six needed between 1,000 and 1,600 calories; the "grown man who pursues a vigorous outdoor life will need from 3500 to 4000." A woman engaged in the heavy labor of housekeeping that included laundry and housecleaning could use 2,500 to 3,000; the "typewriter, stenographer, dressmaker or milliner," leading a more sedentary life, would need only 1,800 to 2,500 calories per day.[69]

To help home cooks navigate the new knowledge, Herrick included a table of calories put together by Gertrude York Christy adapted from *Feeding the Family,* by Mary Swartz Rose, well-known nutritionist and professor at Columbia University's Teachers' College. From this table, readers might learn that a small baking powder biscuit supplied 50 calories and a tablespoon of butter 100 calories. Thus to have a large pat of butter on a small biscuit would mean consuming 150 calories. Adding a dollop of orange marmalade would make it 240 calories. To make it a little easier for novices to plan meals with calories in mind, sample menus for different kinds of people were supplied. Thus a man leading a sedentary life could enjoy a breakfast of fruit, cereal, milk, eggs, or creamed beef on toast (not both), more toast or rolls, butter, and coffee with cream and sugar; the man who could expect a day's worth of "hard muscular work" would have hot cereal, bacon or liver, and bacon or sausage or fish, bread, butter, milk, and coffee with milk and sugar. The difference, calorically, was as little as 60 calories or as great as 500, depending on menu choices. Another calorie-counting cookbook author estimated that the average daily calories required were about 2,200 and divided the day's meals among them, suggesting 500 calories for breakfast, 750 for lunch, and 1,000 for dinner.[70]

In his *Sensible Dieting,* William Engel provided menus for 10 diets, each with a different daily calorie intake. Engel, who warned against "magic diets," noted that "hungering for sympathetic understanding, the fat [people] run amuck from trick diet to trick diet."[71] His menus aimed for balanced meals including fruits and vegetables, as well as proteins and carbohydrates. Not even his lowest calorie diet was completely fat free, and he generously allowed what other diet designers did not: a little cream in the breakfast coffee. Although his diets appear quite sensible, Engel had his bizarre notions, too, claiming that it was a bad idea to drink water with a meal because "water combines with most foods to produce fat. Taken at the table, water also defers digestion, and bad digestion breeds fat." He also rejected exercise as a way to lose weight. Claiming that exercise removes "water in the form of perspiration," Engel argued bizarrely "all the pounds go right back where they came from with the next drink of water."[72]

Lulu Hunt Peters set out to refute the "semi-educated individuals [who] discredit the knowledge of calories, saying that it is a foolish food science, a fallacy, a fetish, and so forth." Particularly, she was angered by those who claimed, "their grandfathers never heard of calories and they got along all right."[73] Recognizing that sometimes progress in human affairs required new language, Peters wanted her readers to think about calories all the time: "Instead of saying one slice of bread, or a piece of pie, you will say 100 calories of bread, 350 calories of pie."[74] Discussing the range of calorie needs relative to age, gender, and occupation, Peters was careful to inform readers: "Mental work does not require added nourishment." Deep thought was not the equivalent of deep knee bends. In fact, she argued that if an excess of calories are taken during mental work, "the work is not so well done."[75]

Although many of the unfounded ideas that appeared in diet books were muddled science and superstition, a blatant example of the misuse of nutritional science came in *Eat and Grow Thin,* a diet book that published "the Mahdah menus," supposedly composed by a European diet expert named Mahdah. The book's author claimed: "The Mahdah menus are based on the dietary charts issued by the USDA (Office of Experimental Stations, Mr. A. C. True, director) and prepared by Mr. C. F. Langworthy, expert in charge of Nutrition Investigations. They furnish the latest and completest statement of food constituents."[76] Using True and Langworthy's well-respected charts of food values, but applying her own logic, "Mahdah provided a list of "forbidden foods" banned because of either fat or carbohydrate content. On the list were such harmless staples as milk, wheat, oats, potatoes, bananas, grapes, walnuts, and raisins. Because *Eat and Grow Thin* republished the charts with only subtle annotations, a reader could easily be misled into thinking that True and Langworthy themselves endorsed this rejection of foods. The tables were actually meant to serve an informational rather than prescriptive purpose, and trained nutritionists would, in any case, advocate a balanced and varied diet, not one that rejected perfectly healthy foods.

At least the Mahdah menus made a virtue of poverty, as Vance Thompson, who wrote the book's introduction cheerfully noted of the menus: "A man at once fat and poor might find some of the dishes beyond his purse. He is to be congratulated, for he will lose flesh just so much more rapidly than his fat and richer brother."[77]

FOOD DURING THE GREAT DEPRESSION

Food became a topic for national discussion during the Great Depression when large numbers of Americans faced hunger and malnutrition despite the fact that farmers were producing enough food to feed the nation. Since before the Great Depression, back as far as the turn of the century, American agriculture had been in transition from family farms to commercial agriculture. Where family farms had produced a variety of crops and livestock to feed a family and some surplus for a local market, commercial farms grew single crops for national and international markets. The transition made it harder and harder for small farms to compete. Those who wanted to make the shift from small scale to large-scale, single-crop farming often had to mortgage their farms to afford the equipment and extra land needed to grow large quantities for large markets. Thus farming conditions were precarious even before the Great Depression struck. When the depression caused widespread unemployment in industrial sectors, consumers who lost income lost buying power, and many farmers found the market for their goods greatly reduced. Ironically, the years between 1929 and 1934 were very productive years on American farms, so there was much to buy but no one to buy it. In fact, prices were so low that it was no longer profitable for farmers to get their goods to market—transportation cost more than they could hope to get from sales. Crop prices dropped 40 percent between 1929 and 1934.

Americans were shocked to hear about surplus crops being destroyed because they could not be brought to market. Milk was spilled into ditches, oranges soaked in kerosene, and cornfields burned down—

all while men, women, and children across the country went hungry. The U.S. government stepped in to try to solve the problem, establishing the Federal Surplus Redistribution Corporation (FSRC) in 1933. The FSRC was supposed to buy surplus crops from farmers and distribute the surplus free to needy families. Their first big effort to do this was a public-relations disaster known as "the slaughter of the little pigs." Hoping to forestall a surplus of hogs on the market in the coming year, the FSRC offered to buy piglets and pregnant sows (called piggy sows) for good prices in 1933. They would then slaughter the pigs and use the meat to feed the unemployed. Slaughter houses were set up to handle larger pigs and many of the piglets escaped, running through the streets of Chicago and immediately drawing the sympathy and outrage of the public. In addition, it proved difficult to get meat to the needy, as distribution networks did not exist. Highly perishable commodities, especially milk, went

A long line of jobless and homeless men wait outside to get free dinner at New York's municipal lodging house in the winter of 1932–33 during the Great Depression. (AP Photo.)

In the early years of the Great Depression, private agencies such as the Salvation army were relied on to give aid to the unemployed. Here, men are fed at a "soup kitchen," January 30, 1934. (AP Photo.)

bad in huge quantities before they could reach the hungry, adding to public fury and not easing stress on desperate families, despite the best efforts of the FSRC. When acute drought struck the Southwest and the topsoil of many family farms simply dried up and blew away, the situation became even worse.

In the early days of the Great Depression, ordinary people in need could turn to local relief agencies and private charities, which at first gave out money to help families feed themselves and then, when requests for help became too numerous, began handing out food. Charities set up commissaries—large centers where food was sold at low cost—but many people felt humiliated to be seen in such places and local merchants complained that these was unfair to their businesses. To complicate matters, relief groceries were given only to families, not to single people, who were thought to be able to fend for themselves.

A list of a week's worth of groceries supplied through an Alabama relief agency is given here:

Relief Receipt from Alabama, 1934

½ lb-meal [powdered grain]	.50
2 boxes oatmeal	.20
5 can milk	.20
10 lbs. sweet potatoes	.30
4 lbs. dried beans	.24
7 oz. can tomatoes	.84
6 lbs. cabbage	.24
3 lbs. dried fruit	.58
3 lbs. onions	.18
6 lbs. lard	.60
1 gal. molasses	.55
4 lbs. meat	.44
1 box salt and one box soda	.10[78]

Many different organizations, institutions, and individuals operated breadlines and soup kitchens where those who waited in long lines could get a single, simple meal. It was noted that even "Gangster Al Capone opened a breadline in Chicago," and someone "calling himself 'Mr. Glad,' gave out coffee, sandwiches, gloves, and nickels in Times Square," in New York.[79]

Much as breadlines were needed to feed the hungry, there was public outcry against them because they made the need of the poor so public. Many thought that these handouts would not help the economy to recover. Meanwhile, the number of people admitted to hospitals suffering from starvation and malnutrition rose steadily.[80] Those who could not get enough help from relief agencies turned to a variety of techniques to feed themselves and their families. Many took to foraging, searching through garbage cans outside of markets and restaurants. Town dumps were frequently crowded with hungry people who waited for trucks to arrive with "fresh" garbage in which they might find something still edible.

Many families who lived in rural or semirural areas foraged for food in the wild, living on berries, mushrooms, and greens. In Philadelphia one family subsisted on dandelion greens between relief allowances.[81] A mining family in Kentucky listed "violet tops, wild onions, forget-me-not, wild lettuce," and whatever weeds cows would eat—the family trusted that cows wouldn't eat anything poisonous—among the foraged foods they regularly consumed.[82]

Author Tillie Olsen, who grew up in Chicago during the Great Depression, remembered being taken to the edge of the city by her mother to forage for wild greens in what was once "someone's good yard." Olsen and her mother and brother gathered nasturtium leaves "only the little ones . . . no bigger'n a penny" until they had "three bags full." They would need a lot, their mother reminded them, because "you know greens boil down to just nothin."[83]

Those who had jobs in the food industry smuggled food home to hungry families. One woman noted that because her father, who worked in a Chinese restaurant, used to bring home fried noodles all the time for the family, she couldn't eat them once the depression ended. When he went to work at a new job delivering breakfast cereals, the family subsisted on Rice Krispies and Cornflakes, both of which also lost their appeal for her.[84] Students lucky enough to get free lunch at school smuggled home some for younger siblings, and women who worked as domestics took home leftovers from their employers' tables.

When food was available, Americans adopted many clever techniques to stretch it as far as they could. Gravy soup, made by browning some flour in a tiny amount of fat and adding water, was a common dish to get families through hard times between more substantive meals.[85] Those who lived in rural and semirural areas planted gardens, carefully timing their plantings so that there would always be something ripe for the family table when there was no other food source to rely on.

Home economists came to the aid of hungry Americans with menus and recipes designed to maximize purchasing power and food value simultaneously. In one nationally distributed bulletin, nutritionists encouraged readers to think of soybeans as a good protein source. Although people in other nations had long relied on soybeans as a dietary staple, Americans had only considered them forage or "food for livestock." The fact was, however, that "some forage crops furnish excellent food for human beings, and this fact now has a new importance in the drought-stricken Middle West." Readers could try them "boiled and seasoned with butter or salt pork; or creamed; or in succotash; or scalloped with tomatoes, corn, and breadcrumbs." Or, if they wanted to risk a little culinary adventure with the new foodstuff: "An oriental way to serve soybeans is to boil the beans in the pods, in water flavored with soy sauce, and serve them to be eaten from the pod."[86] For those struggling to afford food, the nutritionists at the U.S. Bureau of Home Economics recommended making milk a priority grocery, as it supplied many of the body's daily dietary needs and was essential for the health of children.

With basic necessities hard to come by as families took whatever was available from relief agencies or whatever cheap groceries they could afford, government nutritionists did not forget that even desperate people might not eat what did not appeal to them. "It is tremendously important," one Bureau of Home Economics employee wrote, "for us to know what kinds of food we need. Our health depends upon it. But it is doubtful whether all the teaching in the world on that point would keep us on a good diet if we couldn't enjoy the food." For the homemaker charged with making "plain, simple foods inviting," this was an especially hard task "when the family pocketbook limits the choice of food themselves." Careful saving of fat drippings and use of small amounts of sugar, pepper, vinegar, onions, and even the somewhat extravagant curry powder could make cheap nutritious food more exciting.[87]

For the truly desperate, food scientists at Cornell University invented three new foodstuffs, which they called Milkorno, Milkoato, and Milkwheato. The Milk-os were mixtures of grain flour, powdered skim milk, and salt, "an all-around food that has no equal for cheapness and can be used in a dozen different ways."[88] Mixed with water, they could be used as a base for sauces or to stretch small supplies of meat or other proteins. Mixed with eggs and served with syrup, they could take the place of cakes or puddings. The university gave the patent for the flours to the U.S. government so that they could be distributed free to families on relief. Recipes for Milkorno included the resolutely American Milkorno Scrapple and Milkorno Ham Loaf, but also Milkorno Chop Suey, Milkorno Cheese Fondue, and Gnocchi di Milkorno. A recipe for Milkorno Chili is given here.

Milkorno Chili

1 tablespoon fat; 1 pound hamburger; 1 large onion, chopped; 2 cups tomatoes; salt, pepper, and chili powder to taste; 2 cups cooked Milkorno. Brown the onions and hamburger in the fat. Add the tomatoes and seasonings and simmer until the mixture has desired thickness. Add the cooked Milkorno, heat again, and serve.[89]

To publicize the new wonder food, First Lady Eleanor Roosevelt even served Milkorno at the White House. She also made it known that her family would be served a week's worth of the low-cost nutritious meals recommended by home economists for families on relief. As the New York Times reported in March 1933, President Franklin D. Roosevelt and Eleanor Roosevelt had "7½-Cent Economy Luncheons" of "hot stuffed eggs with tomato sauce, mashed potatoes, prune pudding, bread, and coffee," recommended by Cornell University's Department of Home Economics.[90] The president, as was his habit, dined at his desk.

Wartime Needs

When the United States entered World War II in 1941, army doctors were shocked to find that many of the young men who signed up to serve were physically unfit to do so because of nutritional deficiencies. General Lewis Hershey, director of Selective Service, estimated that approximately 133,000 men had been rejected for service because of disabilities directly and indirectly caused by malnutrition, partly because of the hardships of the Great Depression but also the result of generally poor understanding of nutrition and failure to act on what little was understood. President Roosevelt called a Nutrition Conference for National Defense in 1941 to help address this problem.

At the conference, experts in the field of nutrition came together to determine a set of "diet standards" so that public health workers and ordinary Americans might work toward good nutrition. The recommendations were boiled down to one paragraph: "One pint of milk daily for an adult, more for children. One serving of meat. One egg daily or some suitable substitute such as beans. Two servings of vegetable daily, one of which should be green or yellow. Two servings of fruit daily, one of which should be a good source of vitamin C, such as citrus fruits or tomatoes. Bread, flour and cereal, most and preferably all of it whole grain or the new enriched bread, flour and cereals. Some butter or margarine with vitamin A added. Other foods to satisfy the appetite."[91]

Using the worrying information about widespread malnutrition among potential soldiers as a rallying point, conference attendees advocated for a federal school lunch program. If children could be given models of good nutrition in school, as well as being fed, they would grow into healthier adults, or so the experts reasoned. They succeeded in 1946 when Congress established a national school lunch program. Where there had been school lunch programs supplying low-cost nutritious meals to schoolchildren in many states, the National School Lunch Act consolidated all these programs under the Department of Agriculture's Consumer and Marketing Service. The program had a double purpose, giving farmers an outlet for surplus crops and feeding children and potentially teaching them, through eaten examples, the basic principles of nutrition. The school lunch program was required to buy any surplus crops that farmers offered. For the dietitians who planned lunches, as well as the cooks who worked in school cafeterias, this arrangement could be quite inconvenient, as it was impossible to tell from year to year or month to month what crops or meats would be in surplus.

In 1946, the federal government began providing funding for public school lunches. As this 1941 Oklahoma poster shows, states had already started providing lunches, with school dietitians using the opportunity to teach children to think about food groups. (Courtesy of Library of Congress.)

While American soldiers served in the war, attempts were made to provide them with balanced meals in camp and on the battlefield. The most famous result was the K ration, developed by Ancel Keys, a physiologist. Keys was asked by the War Department to come up with a meal that could be carried easily but that would also provide adequate calories to support men in combat. Other rations had been designed for soldiers out of the field of combat and for those in emergency situations. The three meals Keys developed became known as K rations, not after Keys, as is sometimes thought, but simply because the sound was distinct from the other preexisting rations, A, B, and C rations. The three rations—Breakfast, Dinner (Lunch), and Supper— each contained a can of meat product, crackers, some kind of sweet (dried fruit, a chocolate bar, or hard candy), instant coffee, and cigarettes, which were not considered unhealthy at the time.

While men on the front were learning to eat every meal out of a can, their families at home were going without canned foods so that all tin could be used in the war effort. This gave a boost to the sale of frozen foods, packaged as they were in paper.[92] It also meant that when the war ended, civilians were interested in eating canned foods and veterans had grown accustomed to them.

During World War II, Americans were encouraged to grow and preserve their own foods in order to save tin for the war effort. Among other vegetables preserved here are beets, greens, squash, and peas. (Courtesy of Library of Congress.)

On the home front, rationing meant that Americans had to learn to make do with smaller quantities of meat, flour, sugar, and fats, all foodstuffs needed for the army and its allies. In these circumstances, one historian found that women "often called upon the old favorites such as croquettes, hash, jellies, assorted sauces, and 'escalloped' dishes to use up every bit of the increasingly precious meat in the home."[93] Supplies were not the only thing that a home cook might be short of during the war. As one cookbook noted, American women were living on "rationed time," too, as many of them took jobs in the defense industries or volunteered in the war effort. To "save time without sacrificing the cook's poise, the food's value, or the table's charm," this cookbook suggested shortcuts like setting the table in the morning before leaving for work and planning a week's worth of meals in advance.[94] It also offered many recipes that used leftovers to maximize both time and material. More women in the workforce also meant fewer lunches eaten at home. One cookbook offered a chapter on "Wartime Sandwiches"; another recommended paper bags as lunch carriers because, "Many plants insist upon containers that can be inspected as the workers enter and leave the plant."[95] Despite the

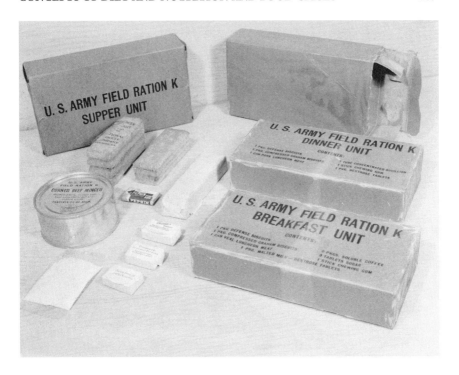

Designed for use in case of emergency, the K ration included crackers, cookies, canned meat (veal, pork, and beef are pictured here), powdered coffee, powdered milk, sugar, and a stick of chewing gum. Some rations included a bouillon cube for making soup. (Courtesy of Library of Congress.)

dainty fare suggested for women's sandwiches in one cookbook, one of the best-known images from the war, Norman Rockwell's "Rosie the Riveter," shows a well-muscled female factory worker eating a hefty sandwich on her lunch break.

On "Meatless Tuesdays," Americans could expect to enjoy such treats as codfish soufflé or a "meatless dinner main dish" of cubed potatoes and peas baked in mushroom sauce.[96] The American Hotel Association Food Supply Committee urged its members to make sure that "variety meat dishes [were] stressed daily," arguing that "Variety meats, including calves' liver, brains, head, pigs' feet, sweetbread, tripe, and kidney can be made into attractive dishes and served at cheaper prices."[97] Families were also encouraged to make "Variety Dishes from the 'odd' cuts" of meat that were not commonly used in mainstream American cuisine. The "Democratic Fricassee," for example, offered in one cookbook, used veal breast, neck, or shoulder, as these were cuts that were not rationed. When more familiar meat,

A woman (left) uses a poster and a "vegetable man" to bring home her message to Dundee, Illinois, housewives at her consumer conservation booth in the West Dundee village hall, 1942. Another woman signs a pledge to avoid food waste. (AP Photo.)

such as beef and pork was available, cooks were told to "Use whole grain cereals" such as oatmeal "as 'filler for stretching meat and vegetable dishes.'" An example of the cuisine of stretching was the recipe for "Military Meatballs" that included a high proportion of bread and the "Victory Medley."[98]

Victory Medley

4 ounces (½ package) noodles, ½ lb sausage, 1 cup whole kernel corn, 1 can tomato sauce, ½ lb grated cheese, 1 cup ripe olives, 1 tbsp minced parsley, ½ tsp celery salt, ½ tsp onion salt, ⅛ tsp pepper, 1 can condensed mushroom or tomato soup. Cook noodles in salted water and drain. Cook sausage until brown and crumbly; pour off fat. Do not drain corn. Save 1 cup cheese for top. Mix all other ingredients and pour into a greased 2-quart casserole. Top with cheese. Bake at 350° F for 1 hour. Serves 6 to 8.[99]

In 1944, *Good Housekeeping Magazine* reported that the war had brought changes to the lifestyles of the well-to-do: "In California 'help-less' hostesses are pioneering in a new kind of entertaining. They're reducing party menus to the fundamentals of a hearty, old-timey soup such as their covered-wagon grandmothers might have made, plus a salad, bread, and sometimes dessert."[100] As servants quit for the higher wages available in defense jobs, women of leisure were forced to pioneer a new, more relaxed style. Home cooks were also reminded that "there is no ration on garnishes!" so meals need not lose all their aesthetic appeal.[101]

RELIGION AND FOOD

Dietary restrictions have never played a big role in the practice of Protestant Christianity in North America. Occasional communal fast days, invoked by leaders in earlier eras, were no longer community events by the end of the 19th century. Although Catholics abstained from meat on Fridays in the period of Lent, fewer and fewer also did so throughout the year. One small group who mixed diet and religion were Seventh Day Adventists who were encouraged by their leadership to be vegetarian and also to adhere to dietary restrictions similar to those practiced by orthodox Jews. Members of the Church of the Latter Day Saints, also known as Mormons, ate typical American fare but refused drinks with caffeine or alcohol.

Between 1880 and 1924, approximately 2 million Jewish immigrants, mostly from Eastern Europe, arrived in America. With them they brought a distinct cuisine that required specialty stores such as kosher butchers and matzo bakeries. Before this largest wave of Jewish immigration, approximately a quarter of a million Americans were of Jewish ancestry, most of those descended from German immigrants and mostly leading largely secular lives. The new immigrants tended to hold more closely to Jewish dietary restrictions, but they were also eager to assimilate into American culture. Many women from these communities attended cooking classes in urban settlement houses, and they formed an eager audience for cookbooks in both Yiddish and English. Both settlement house cooking classes and cookbooks written for a Jewish audience often blended traditional Eastern European dishes with those of American cuisine. Some were kosher, but many were not.[102]

One of the best-known cookbooks of the era was *The Settlement Cook Book,* which was the result of cooking classes offered in a Milwaukee, Wisconsin settlement house. This book offered recipes for matzo schalet (a pudding made with matzos soaked in goose fat) but also for lobster Newburg, shrimp wiggles, and boiled ham, all forbidden by Jewish dietary laws. To further emphasize the fact that this was a book for those who wanted to adopt their new culture, even if still cooking a few treats from the old, a chapter on "Household Rules" did not include any information about how to keep a kosher kitchen.

Florence Kreisler Greenbaum's *International Jewish Cook Book,* published in 1918, was much truer to ancient traditions of Jewish cooking, offering not only recipes "according to Jewish dietary laws," but also instructions on the "the rules for kashering" or making kosher, one's kitchen. Greenbaum was introduced to the reader as both modern and traditional. She had studied food chemistry at Hunter College, but "many of these recipes have been used in her household for three generations," so readers could be sure that there was nothing too radically new in the book.[103]

The yearning for familiar foods could determine a family's fate, as in the case of the Orensteins, a family described by historian Hasia Diner. Joe Orenstein was happy farming in rural Ohio, remote from Jewish culture, but his wife Bertha insisted that they move to a city, saying, "I can't live like this. I just can't do it. There isn't even a bit of kosher food." The family moved to a city where, as Diner recounts, "Bertha could get her ritually approved foods."[104] For other immigrants, the abundance and variety of nonkosher foods available in America proved hard to resist. In *The Rise of David Levinsky,* a young Jewish immigrant to New York finds that "the very clothes I wore and the very food I ate had a fatal effect on my religious habits," and that many of the Jews he met in New York "openly patronized Gentile restaurants and would not hesitate even to eat pork."[105] As America became a more obviously multicultural society, even non-Jews learned to appreciate the availability of a kosher butcher. In their 1914 cookbook, *How to Cook and Why,* Elizabeth Condit and Jessie Long, both instructors in Pratt Institute's Household Science Department, noted that "in cities or towns where there are orthodox Jewish (kosher) markets the buyer can always be sure to get fresh-killed poultry, as no cold-storage poultry may be sold in such markets."[106] One man's failure to assimilate was another's fresh meat.

NOTES

1. "13,000 Dispeptics in Lima," *Lima (Ohio) Daily News,* June 2, 1913, p. 5.

2. "Capsular Diet and Scientific Menu Cards—Are They Doomed?" *New York Times,* March 6, 1904, p. 26.

3. "Dietary Theorists," *New York Times,* November 8, 1904, p. 8.

4. Advertisement, *New York Times,* April 27, 1890, p. 13; Advertisement, *Alton (Illinois) Telegraph,* January 1, 1891, p. 2; *Lima (Ohio) Daily News* January 1, 1895, p. 3; Advertisement, *New York Times,* January 4, 1910, p. 7.

5. "Popularity of Diets," *New York Evening Sun,* reprinted in the *(Lincoln) Nebraska State Journal,* March 27, 1910, p. 4.

6. Agricola (pseudonym for unknown author) "Day by Day," *(Des Moines) Iowa Homestead,* May 26, 1910, p. 10.

7. Horace Fletcher, *The New Glutton or Epicure* (New York: F. A. Stokes, 1906), p. 308.

8. Fletcher, *The New Glutton or Epicure,* p. 313.

9. Harvey Levenstein, *Revolution at the Table* (Berkeley: University of California Press, 2003), p. 89.

10. Carl Malmberg, *Diet and Die* (New York: Hilman Curl, 1935).

11. Hay, *Health Via Food* (East Aurora, NY: Sun-Diet Health Service, Inc., 1929), p. 19.

12. Hay, *Health Via Food,* p. 290.

13. Hay, *Health Via Food,* p. 28.

14. Oliver Cabana, Introduction to William Howard Hay, *Health Via Food,* p. 14.

15. Hay, *Health Via Food,* p. 261.

16. Hay, *Health Via Food,* pp. 261, 262.

17. Hay, *Health Via Food,* p. 260.

18. Hay, *Health Via Food,* p. 297.

19. Malmberg, *Diet and Die,* pp. 68–69.

20. Malmberg, *Diet and Die,* p. 71.

21. Edna Ferber, *Roast Beef Medium* (New York: Frederick A. Stokes Company, 1913), p. 89.

22. "Blair," "Seasonable Cookery," *Delineator,* November 1897, 50, no. 5, p. 599.

23. "Cream Celery Soup," *The Times Cook Book No. 2* (Los Angeles: Times-Mirror Co., 1905), p. 14.

24. "Cream Celery Soup," p. 33.

25. *The Vegetarian* 1, no. 1 (July 15, 1895): 10.

26. *The Vegetarian* 1, no. 3 (September 15, 1895): 42–43.

27. Thetta Quay Franks, *Daily Menus for War Service* (New York: G. P. Putnam's Sons, 1918), p. 4.

28. Franks, *Daily Menus for War Service,* p. 32.

29. Franks, *Daily Menus for War Service,* p. 35.

30. Jean Robert Albert, "Charity a Menace—An Insult," *Vegetarian Fruitarian Humanitarian,* 35, no. 6 (June, 1935): 18.

31. Fannie Hurst, *No Food with My Meals* (New York: Harper & Brothers Publishers, 1935), pp. 11–12.

32. Advertisements, *Delineator,* 7, no. 6 (Early Summer 1896): 636, x.

33. B. Johnston, *Eat and Grow Fat* (New York: The Sherwood Company, 1917), p. 5.

34. Johnston, *Eat and Grow Fat,* p. 6.

35. Johnston, *Eat and Grow Fat,* p. 35.

36. Johnston, *Eat and Grow Fat,* p. 20.

37. Leona M. Bayer, M.D., and Edith S. Green, *Kitchen Strategy: Vitamin Values Made Easy. What? Why? How? To Feed Your Family* (San Francisco: Lithotype Process Company, 1943), p. 39.

38. Marion Harland, *The New Common Sense in the Household* (New York: Frederick A. Stokes Company, 1926), pp. 498–99.

39. Advertisement, *Sears Roebuck Catalog, 1935,* pp. 771, 773.

40. Malmberg, *Diet and Die,* p. 123.

41. Malmberg, *Diet and Die,* p. 125.

42. Hurst, *No Food With My Meals,* p. 50.

43. Malmberg, *Diet and Die,* pp. 95–96.

44. Malmberg, *Diet and Die,* p. 96.

45. Malberg, *Diet and Die,* p. 98.

46. William Engel, *Sensible Dieting* (New York: Alfred A. Knopf, 1939), pp. ix–x.

47. Mariposa, *Hollywood Glamour Cook Book* (Miami, FL: Glamour Publications, 1940), p. 76.

48. Mariposa, *Hollywood Glamour Cook Book,* pp. 86, 91.

49. Mariposa, *Hollywood Glamour Cook Book,* p. 291.

50. A. B. Johnston, *Eat and Grow Slender* (New York: R. E. Sherwood, 1916), p. 5.

51. Johnston, *Eat and Grow Slender,* pp. 17, 19.

52. "Warning Is Issued against Freak Diets," *Galveston Texas Daily News,* September 21, 1913, p. 28.

53. Dr. Thomas Jay Allen, "Houston's Advice to 'Eat What You Want,' Is Attacked by a Physician," *Washington (D.C.) Post,* October 5, 1913, p. 23.

54. Albert S. Gray, "Fundamental Principles of Health," *Stevens Point (Wisconsin) Daily Journal,* January 23, 1915, p. 9.

55. Patricia Drubber, *Vitamins and Calories* (Washington, D.C.: The Washington Service Bureau, 1942), p. 4.

56. Walter Hollis Eddy, *The Vitamine Manual* (Philadelphia: Williams & Wilkins Company, 1921), p. 85.

57. Mrs. S. T. Rorer, "What Rheumatic People Should Eat," *Ladies Home Journal,* 24, no. 3 (February, 1907): 348.

58. Rorer, "What Rheumatic People Should Eat," p. 348.

59. Ellen Richards, *Plain Words About Food: The Rumford Kitchen Leaflets* (Boston: Rockwell and Churchill, 1899).

60. Elizabeth Lay Green, *Balanced Diet: A One-Act Comedy* (New York: Samuel French, 1928), p. 23.

61. Casimir Funk, Introduction to C. Houston Goudiss, *Eating Vitamines* (New York: Funk & Wagnalls Company, 1922), p. xi.

62. C. Houston Goudiss, *Eating Vitamines* (New York: Funk & Wagnalls Company, 1922), p. 3.

63. Goudiss, *Eating Vitamines,* p. 25.

64. Prudence Penny, *Coupon Cookery* (Hollywood, CA: Murray & Gee, Inc., 1943), p. 22.

65. I. M. Ornburn, *Nutrition and Labor* (Washington, D.C.: Union Label Trades Department, 1942), p. 5.

66. Hurst, *No Food with My Meals,* p. 52.

67. Malmberg, *Diet and Die,* p. 23.

68. Engel, *Sensible Dieting,* p. 10.

69. Marion Harland, *The New Common Sense in the Household* (New York: Frederick A. Stokes Company, 1926), p. 487.

70. Franks, *Daily Menus for War Service,* p. 3.

71. Engel, *Sensible Dieting,* p. 85.

72. Engel, *Sensible Dieting,* p. 80.

73. Dr. Lulu Hunt Peters, *Diet and Health with Key to the Calories* (Chicago: The Reilly and Lee Co., 1918), p. 23.

74. Peters, *Diet and Health with Key to the Calories,* p. 24.

75. Peters, *Diet and Health with Key to the Calories,* p. 25.

76. Vance Thompson, *Eat and Grow Thin: The Mahdah Menus* (New York: E. P. Dutton & Company Publishers, 1914), p. 94.

77. Vance Thompson, "Introduction," *The Mahdah Menus,* p. 16.

78. Relief grocery list from the Alabama State Archives, http://www.archives.state.al.us/teacher/dep/dep4/doc1.html (accessed February 12, 2009).

79. Janet Poppendeik, *Breadlines Knee-deep in Wheat* (New Brunswick, NJ: Rutgers University Press, 1986), p. 25.

80. Poppendeik, *Breadlines Knee-deep in Wheat,* pp. 31–32.

81. Poppendeik, *Breadlines Knee-deep in Wheat,* p. 26.

82. Poppendeik, *Breadlines Knee-deep in Wheat,* p. 31.

83. Tillie Olsen *Yonnondio: From the Thirties* (Lincoln: University of Nebraska Press, 2004), pp. 143, 145.

84. Poppendeik, *Breadlines Knee-deep in Wheat,* p. 27.

85. Poppendeik, *Breadlines Knee-deep in Wheat,* p. 31.

86. *The Market Basket: Green Soybeans as a Vegetable,* September 5, 1934, p. 2.

87. *The Market Basket: Cheap Seasonings for the Low-Cost Meal,* November 14, 1934, pp. 1–4.

88. "Meals for a Family of 5 for $5 a Week," Undated clipping from unidentified newspaper, exhibited in "What Was Home Economics?" online exhibition: http://rmc.library.cornell.edu/homeEc/4impact/milkorno.html (accessed July 30, 2008).

89. "What Was Home Economics?" online exhibition: http://rmc.library.cornell.edu/homeEc/4impact/milkorno3.html (accessed July 30, 2008).

90. "7½-cent Economy Luncheons Served to the Roosevelts," *New York Times,* March 22, 1933, p. 9.

91. "Diet Standards for Americans of All Ages Announced," *The Science News-Letter,* 39, no. 22 (May, 1941): 347–48.

92. Eldon Bernstein and Fred Carstensen, "Rising to the Occasion: Lender's Bagels and the Frozen Food Revolution, 1927–1985," *Business and Economic History,* 25, no. 1 (1996): 167.

93. Jessamyn Neuhaus, *Manly Meals and Mom's Home Cooking* (Baltimore: The Johns Hopkins University Press, 2003), p. 109.

94. Leona M. Bayer, M.D., and Edith S. Green, *Kitchen Strategy: Vitamin Values Made Easy. What? Why? How? To Feed Your Family* (San Francisco: Lithotype Process Company, 1943), p. 100.

95. Marion Gregg, ed., *The American Women's Voluntary Services Cook Book: A Book for Wartime Living* (San Francisco: Recorder Sunset Press, 1942); Prudence Penny, *Coupon Cookery* (Hollywood, CA: Murray & Gee, Inc., 1943), p. 98.

96. Judith Wilson, "Codfish Souffle Served as Satisfying Main Dish," *Hayward (California) Daily Review,* January 29, 1942, p. 2; "Main Dish," *Sheboygan (Wisconsin) Journal,* February 5, 1942, p. 21.

97. "A.H.A. Cooperates with Government Share-the-Meat Campaign," *Hotel Monthly,* 50, no. 596 (November 1942), cited in *Journal of Home Economics,* 35, no. 3 (March 1943): 184.

98. Prudence Penny, *Coupon Cookery* (Hollywood, CA: Murray & Gee, 1943), pp. 36, 46, 50, 51.

99. Penny, *Coupon Cookery,* p. 64.

100. *Good Housekeeping,* 18, no. 1 (January 1944): 84.

101. Penny, *Coupon Cookery,* p. 115.

102. Hasia Diner, *Hungering for America* (Cambridge, MA: Harvard University Press, 2001), p. 217.

103. Florence Kreisler Greenbaum, *International Jewish Cook Book,* (New York: Bloch Publishing Company, 1918), first page after title, no page number.

104. Diner, *Hungering for America,* p. 183.

105. Abraham Cahan, *The Rise of David Levinsky* (New York: Harper and Brothers Publishers, 1917), p. 110.

106. Elizabeth Condit and Jessie A. Long, *How to Cook and Why* (New York: Harper and Brothers Publishers, 1914), p. 161.

SELECTED BIBLIOGRAPHY

Abel, Mary Hinman. *Practical, Sanitary and Economic Cooking Adapted to Persons of Moderate and Small Means.* Rochester, NY: American Public Health Association, 1890.

Algren, Nelson. *America Eats.* Iowa City: University of Iowa Press, 1992.

Allen, Ida Bailey. *Double-Quick Cooking for Part-Time Homemakers.* New York: M. Barrows and Company, 1943.

Allen, Ida Bailey, *Mrs. Allen on Cooking, Menus, Service: 2500 Recipes.* Garden City, NY: Doubleday Page, 1924.

Allen, Lucy G. *Choice Recipes for Clever Cooks.* Boston: Little, Brown, and Company, 1924.

Bache, Elizabeth DuBois. *When Mother Lets Us Make Candy.* New York: Moffat, Yard and Co., 1915.

Bayer, Leona M., M.D., and Edith S. Green. *Kitchen Strategy.* San Francisco: Lithotype Process Company, 1943.

Belasco, Warren, and Philip Scranton. *Food Nations.* New York: Routledge, 2002.

Bentley, Mildred Maddocks. *Good Housekeeping's Book on the Business of Housekeeping.* New York: Good Housekeeping, 1924.

Bosse, Sara. *Chinese-Japanese Cook Book.* Chicago: Rand McNally, 1914.

Bradley, Alice. *Cooking for Profits: Catering and Food Service Management.* Chicago: American School of Home Economics, 1925.

Brobeck, Florence. *Cook It in a Casserole.* New York: M. Barrows and Company, 1943.

Brown, Clair. *American Standards of Living, 1918–1988.* New York: HarperCollins, 1994.

Byington, Margaret. *Homestead: The Households of a Mill Town.* New York: Russell Sage Foundation, 1910.

Cazaux, Douglas. *Orange Empire: California and the Fruits of Eden*. Berkeley: University of California Press, 2005.

Chapin, Robert Coit. *The Standard of Living Among Workingmen's Families in New York City*. New York: Russell Sage Foundation Charities Publication Committee, 1909.

Colquitt, Harriet Ross. *The Savannah Cook Book*. New York: Farar & Rinehart, 1933.

Condit, Elizabeth, and Jessie A. Long. *How to Cook and Why*. New York: Harper and Brothers Publishers, 1914.

Cowan, Ruth Schwartz. *More Work for Mother*. New York: Basic Books, 1983.

DeBoth, Jessie Marie. *Modern Guide to Better Meals*. Chicago: Cuneo Press, 1939.

De Knight, Freda. *A Date with a Dish: A Cook Book of American Negro Recipes*. New York: Hermitage Press, 1948.

Dennison, Grace E. *The American Home Cook Book*. New York: Grosset & Dunlap, 1932.

Diner, Hasia. *Hungering for America*. Cambridge, MA: Harvard University Press, 2001.

Drubber, Patricia. *Vitamins and Calories*. Washington, D.C.: The Washington Service Bureau, 1942.

Eddy, Walter Hollis. *The Vitamine Manual*. Philadelphia: Williams & Wilkins Company, 1921.

Elias, Megan. *Stir It Up: Home Economics in American Culture*. Philadelphia: University of Pennsylvania Press, 2008.

Engel, William. *Sensible Dieting*. New York: Alfred A. Knopf, 1939.

Estes, Rufus. *Good Things to Eat*. Chicago: The Author, 1911.

Farmer, Fannie Merritt. *The Boston Cooking-School Cook Book*. Boston: Little, Brown, and Company, 1896.

Fletcher, Horace. *The New Glutton or Epicure*. New York: F. A. Stokes, 1906.

Franks, Thetta Quay. *Daily Menus for War Service*. New York: G. P. Putnam's Sons, 1918.

Gabaccia, Donna. *We Are What We Eat*. Cambridge, MA: Harvard University Press, 1998.

Green, Elizabeth Lay. *Balanced Diet: A One-act Comedy*. New York: Samuel French, 1928.

Greenbaum, Florence Kreisler. *International Jewish Cook Book*. New York: Bloch Publishing Company, 1918.

Gregg, Marion, ed., *The American Women's Voluntary Services Cook Book: A Book for Wartime Living*. San Francisco: Recorder Sunset Press, 1942.

Goudiss, C. Houston. *Eating Vitamines*. New York: Funk & Wagnalls Company, 1922.

Hackney, Mrs. G. Edgar. *Dining for Moderns*. New York: The New York Exchange for Women's Work, 1940.

Harland, Marion. *The New Common Sense in the Household*. New York: Frederick A. Stokes Company, 1926.

Hay, William Howard. *Health Via Food*. East Aurora, NY: Sun-Diet Health Service, 1929.

Herrick, Christine Terhune. *Consolidated Library of Modern Cooking and Household Recipes*. New York: J. H. Bodmer Company, 1904.

Hill, Janet M. *Salads, Sandwiches and Chafing Dish Dainties*. Boston: Little, Brown, and Company, 1914.

Hill, Janet McKenzie. *The American Cook Book*. Boston: Boston Cooking-School Magazine, 1914.

Hines, Duncan. *Adventures in the Art of Good Cooking*. Bowling Green, KY: Adventures in Good Eating, 1939.

The Home Institute of the New York Herald Tribune. *America's Cook Book*. New York: Charles Scribner's Sons, 1937.

Horowitz, David. *Putting Meat on the American Table*. Baltimore: Johns Hopkins University Press, 2006.

Hurst, Fannie. *No Food With My Meals*. New York: Harper & Brothers Publishers, 1935.

Jakle, John A. and Keith A. Sculle. *Fast Food*. Baltimore: The Johns Hopkins University Press, 1999.

Jennings, Linda Deziah. *Washington Women's Cookbook*. Seattle: Washington Equal Suffrage Association, 1909.

Johnston, B. *Eat and Grow Fat*. New York: The Sherwood Company, 1917.

Johnston, B. *Eat and Grow Slender*. New York: R. E. Sherwood, 1916.

Kingsland, Mrs. Burton. *The Book of Weddings*. Garden City, NY: Doubleday, Page & Co., 1907.

Kobler, John. *Ardent Spirits: The Rise and Fall of Prohibition*. New York: Da Capo Press, 1993.

Kyrk, Hazel. *A Theory of Consumption*. Boston: Houghton, Mifflin Co., 1923.

The Ladies of the Jennings Avenue Methodist Episcopal Church, comp. and ed. *The Twentieth Century Home and Cook Book*. Cleveland, OH, 1903.

Levenstein, Harvey. *A Revolution at the Table*. Berkeley: University of California Press, 2003.

Lifshey, Earl. *The Housewares Story*. Chicago: National Housewares Manufacturers Association, 1973.

Malmberg, Carl. *Diet and Die*. New York: Hilman Curl, 1935.

Mariposa. *Hollywood Glamour Cook Book*. Miami, FL: Glamour Publications, 1940.

Matthews, Mary Lockwood. *Foods and Cookery and the Care of the House*. Boston: Little, Brown, and Company, 1921.

Meyerson, Abraham. *The Nervous Housewife*. Boston: Little, Brown, 1920.

Murray, Sarah. *Moveable Feasts*. New York: St. Martin's Press, 2007.

Neil, Marion Harris. *Favorite Recipes Cook Book*. New York: Wiley, 1931.

Neuhaus, Jessamyn. *Manly Meals and Mom's Home Cooking*. Baltimore: The Johns Hopkins University Press, 2003.

Ornburn, I. M. *Nutrition and Labor*. Washington, D.C.: Union Label Trades Department, 1942.

Paddleford, Clementine. *How America Eats*. New York: Charles Scribner's Sons, 1960.

Panschar, William G. *Baking in America*. Vol. 1, *Economic Development*. Evanston, IL: Northwestern University Press, 1956.

Penny, Prudence. *Coupon Cookery*. Hollywood, CA: Murray & Gee, 1943.

Peters, Dr. Lulu Hunt. *Diet and Health with Key to the Calories*. Chicago: The Reilly and Lee Co., 1918.

Pierce, Paul. *Suppers*. Chicago: Brewer, Barse & Co., 1907.

Poppendeik, Janet. *Breadlines Knee-deep in Wheat*. New Brunswick, NJ: Rutgers University Press, 1986.

Post, Emily. *Etiquette in Society, Business, Politics and at Home*. New York: Funk & Wagnalls Company, 1922.

Richards, Ellen. *Plain Words About Food: The Rumford Kitchen Leaflets*. Boston: Rockwell and Churchill, 1899.

Rider, Fremont, ed. *Rider's New York City*. New York: Henry Holt and Company, 1916.

Robertson, Helen, Sarah MacLeod, and Frances Preston. *What Do We Eat Now?* Philadelphia: J. B. Lippincott Company, 1942.

Sangster, Margaret E. *Good Manners for All Occasions*. New York: Cupples & Leon Company, 1921.

Schwartz, Hillel. *Never Satisfied*. New York: Anchor Books, 1986.

Scott, Rhea C. *Home Labor Saving Devices*. Philadelphia: J. B. Lippincott Company, 1917.

Senn, Herman. *Chafing Dish and Casserole Cookery*. London: The Food and Cookery Publishing Company, 1918.

Smith, Andrew. *Pure Ketchup: A History of America's Favorite Condiment*. Columbia: University of South Carolina Press, 1996.

Stewart, Elinore Pruitt. *Letters of A Woman Homesteader*. Boston: Houghton Mifflin Company, 1914.

Thompson, Vance. *Eat and Grow Thin: The Mahdah Menus*. New York: E. P. Dutton & Company Publishers, 1914.

Tomes, Nancy. *The Gospel of Germs*. Cambridge, MA: Harvard University Press, 1998.

van Willigen, John, and Anne van Willigen. *Food and Everyday Life on Kentucky Family Farms*. Lexington: The University of Kentucky Press, 2006.

Vulte, Hermann T. *Food Industries*. Easton, PA: The Chemical Publishing Co., 1920.

Williams, Martha McCulloch. *Dishes and Beverages of the Old South*. New York, McBride, Nast & Company 1913.

INDEX

About the Author

MEGAN J. ELIAS is assistant professor of history at Queensborough Community College, Bayside, New York. She is the author of *Stir It Up: Home Economics in American Culture.*